Dream Interpretation and Spiritual Cleansing

Unveiling the Mysteries of Your Psyche and Purifying Your Energy for Clarity and Peace

© Copyright 2024 – All rights reserved.

The content contained within this book may not be reproduced, duplicated or transmitted without direct written permission from the author or the publisher.

Under no circumstances will any blame or legal responsibility be held against the publisher, or author, for any damages, reparation, or monetary loss due to the information contained within this book, either directly or indirectly.

Legal Notice:

This book is copyright protected. It is only for personal use. You cannot amend, distribute, sell, use, quote or paraphrase any part, or the content within this book, without the consent of the author or publisher.

Disclaimer Notice:

Please note the information contained within this document is for educational and entertainment purposes only. All effort has been executed to present accurate, up to date, reliable, complete information. No warranties of any kind are declared or implied. Readers acknowledge that the author is not engaging in the rendering of legal, financial, medical or professional advice. The content within this book has been derived from various sources. Please consult a licensed professional before attempting any techniques outlined in this book.

By reading this document, the reader agrees that under no circumstances is the author responsible for any losses, direct or indirect, that are incurred as a result of the use of information contained within this document, including, but not limited to, errors, omissions, or inaccuracies.

Your Free Gift
(only available for a limited time)

Thanks for getting this book! If you want to learn more about various spirituality topics, then join Mari Silva's community and get a free guided meditation MP3 for awakening your third eye. This guided meditation mp3 is designed to open and strengthen ones third eye so you can experience a higher state of consciousness. Simply visit the link below the image to get started.

https://spiritualityspot.com/meditation

Or, Scan the QR code!

Table of Contents

PART 1: DREAM INTERPRETATION 1
   INTRODUCTION 2
   CHAPTER 1: WHY DO WE DREAM? 4
   CHAPTER 2: REMEMBER YOUR DREAMS AND LOOK FOR PATTERNS 14
   CHAPTER 3: WHAT ARE YOU DOING IN YOUR DREAM? 24
   CHAPTER 4: DREAM LOCATIONS AND MEANINGS 34
   CHAPTER 5: DREAM SYMBOLISM OF THE FOUR ELEMENTS 43
   CHAPTER 6: LOOKING AT COLORS AND NUMBERS 55
   CHAPTER 7: DREAMS WITH ANIMALS AND PLANTS 68
   CHAPTER 8: DREAMS ABOUT BODY PARTS 79
   CHAPTER 9: WHEN SUPERNATURAL BEINGS APPEAR 88
   CHAPTER 10: ADVANCED DREAM INTERPRETATION TECHNIQUES 96
   GLOSSARY OF DREAM SYMBOLS 104
   CONCLUSION 111
PART 2: SPIRITUAL CLEANSING 113
   INTRODUCTION 114
   CHAPTER 1: YOU AND YOUR SPIRITUAL WELFARE 116
   CHAPTER 2: YOUR AURA AND CHAKRAS 101 125
   CHAPTER 3: CLEANSING YOUR AURA AND CHAKRAS 136
   CHAPTER 4: MEDITATION TO RAISE YOUR VIBRATION 146
   CHAPTER 5: THE HEALING POWER OF REIKI 155

CHAPTER 6: CLEANSING ENERGY WITH REIKI 166
CHAPTER 7: TO SMUDGE OR NOT TO SMUDGE 175
CHAPTER 8: SPIRITUAL BATHS FOR CLEANSING AND PROTECTION 186
CHAPTER 9: CRYSTAL PURIFICATION AND PROTECTION 197
CHAPTER 10: CLEANSING AND PROTECTING YOUR LOVED ONES 206
GLOSSARY OF USEFUL HERBS 215
CONCLUSION 220
HERE'S ANOTHER BOOK BY MARI SILVA THAT YOU MIGHT LIKE 222
YOUR FREE GIFT (ONLY AVAILABLE FOR A LIMITED TIME) 223
BIBLIOGRAPHY 224
IMAGE SOURCES 236

Part 1: Dream Interpretation

A Spiritual Guide to Symbols, Words, Themes, and Meanings of Dreams

Introduction

Due to their elusive and mysterious nature, dreams have always interested people. Since ancient times, different civilizations have wondered why people dream and what these dreams could mean. They recorded their interpretations and used dream symbolism for healing, divination, and guidance. At the beginning of the twentieth century, people started to take a more scientific approach to dream interpretation. From this book, you will learn the different theories about the role of dream symbolism in psychoanalysis and how these can be incorporated into traditional beliefs about dreams.

While there is no clear answer to whether a dream means anything, looking into your dream—including its elements and circumstances—can give you a better idea of how to interpret it. Sometimes, the information you uncover about yourself in your sleep is far more substantial than what you learn during waking hours. Dreams can echo consolidated memories you have had, stimuli your brain has trouble processing in REM sleep, and much more. To find a connection between your dream state and waking life, you'll need to start by taking note of what you've experienced in your dreams—and this book will help you through comprehensive explanations and beginner-friendly practical advice.

For example, your dreams can involve specific actions, locations, elements, colors, or numbers. You can also have recurring dreams about body parts, plants, animals, and even supernatural beings. From spiritual guides to fairies and dwarves, there is no limit to what your imagination can conjure up in your dreams. The book has chapters dedicated to all these possible dream elements, discussing their meanings, variations, and significance in waking life. Still, since dreams stem from the subconscious mind, no symbol can have definitive, universal importance. In the last chapter, you'll learn a few advanced dream interpretation techniques to provide more detailed insight into your dreams and their connection to your waking life.

The key to a successful dream interpretation is to avoid interpreting them literally. While the symbols can hint at which direction you should be heading with your analysis, what truly matters is your emotional connection to your dreams. Decoding the emotions each dream evokes allows you to expand your consciousness. Your dreams are extensions of the subconscious mind, and you are increasing your emotional and spiritual awareness with each dream you interpret. Creating a conscious mental catalog of the meaning of your dreams is like learning a new language. And just like when learning a new language, you embark on a rewarding journey. Read on if you're ready to start deciphering your dreams and earning the ultimate rewards that come with them.

Chapter 1: Why Do We Dream?

Dreams are a mystery humanity has been exploring since the dawn of time. This chapter is designed to answer the question posed in the title from the perspective of various fields of study: Scientific, psychological, religious, and spiritual. It will define the dream interpretation concept and explore its historical and cultural context and benefits. You will also learn about the different types of dreams.

The Concept of Dream Interpretation

The origins of dream interpretation can be traced back to 3000-4000 B.C. to ancient Babylon and Samaria. These civilizations used clay tablets to record people's dreams and interpret their possible meanings. While nothing tangible supports this, historians believe that the Sumerians and the Babylonians believed that dreams were the extension of real life. Some archeological evidence suggests that the Sumerians saw the dream realm as a far more powerful world than the waking one. They saw dreams as a way to liberate and empower themselves because all things are possible in dreams, and a person can do more than they can in real life.

In ancient Greece and ancient Rome, troops heading to the battlefield were often accompanied by dream interpreters who tried to discern the upcoming fight's outcome based on the warriors' dreams. They considered dreams as messages from the gods, often formulated as orders people had to follow.

In ancient Egypt, Pharos and other leaders also relied on dream interpretation when making critical decisions. The Egyptian interpreters recorded people's dreams in hieroglyphics. If someone had particularly vivid dreams or events in their dreams that affected their waking life, they were believed to be blessed by the gods. Dream interpreters were held in high regard as they were said to be divinely gifted by the gods.

The Bible has over 700 references to dreams and their significance in the waking world.

A prophecy was one of the biggest reasons dream interpretation was widespread in all different cultures. Most of the time, people analyze dreams for signs of warnings about the future. Whatever the source of the warning messages, they were seen as hints about future events. Even better, people discovered that dreams offered advice on what to do or avoid when challenging situations arose. At other times, dreams were messages from evil spirits, demons, and other creatures—threats people were made aware of and advised to protect themselves against in their sleep.

Dream interpretations were also used for medicinal purposes, especially in ancient China and ancient Greece. They could help establish a proper diagnosis and treatment plan for an illness and determine what was wrong with the dreamer's body or mind.

The ancient Chinese believed dreams were souls of resting people expressing their desires. According to the Chinese, after the body fell asleep, the soul left it and ventured into the dream realm. People were warned not to suddenly wake someone, as this could cause their souls to remain trapped in the dream world. Even contemporary Chinese people choose to wake up naturally and avoid using alarm locks.

Mexican and Native American tribes also view dreams as the dimension of a soul. Their ancestors live in the dream world, appearing as other living forms, like plants or animals. They use the dream world to visit and communicate with ancestral spirits. In dreams, the ancestors can help answer questions, share wisdom about life, and offer guidance for finding one's path.

Later on, the popularity of dream interpretation diminished drastically—and by the nineteenth century, dreams were dismissed as signifiers of real-life events. Dreams were attributed to indigestion, anxiety, or a noisy environment at night. It was not until the early twentieth century that dream analysis was revived by Austrian psychoanalyst Sigmund Freud.

While treating mental illnesses, Freud realized that his patients' dreams had significance when finding the treatment for their condition. By analyzing their dreams, he helped patients understand the cause of their mental health issues. He believed that by using the information the patients revealed in their dream, he could find a way to cure or manage their symptoms.

Ever since then, this discipline has grown increasingly popular. Soon after Freud, other psychoanalysts and medical professionals became interested in dream interpretation. Ann Faraday, the author of the novel *The Dream Game*, writes about many dream interpretation techniques. Nowadays, dream research continues to grow. However, researchers often encounter a common problem: How to memorize dream images. Unless people find their dreams intellectually stimulating, joyful, or inspiring, they often forget what they dream about the moment they wake up.

Others believe your dreams can reveal more about yourself than the meaning of the dream itself. This is based on a modern scientific approach, which suggests that dreams are the brain's response to external stimuli, which the organ cannot process during waking hours. This contradicts the popular theory of dreams being the gateway for hidden desires. Another issue with dream interpretation is that you are more likely to remember your dreams if they revolve around adverse events or circumstances surrounding people you dislike. While you can also retain dreams related to loved ones and other positive dreams, the percentage is far less than retained negative dreams. This means that you will likely interpret dreams so that they can support your beliefs about your environment, yourself, and other people.

People who often rely on dream interpretation for orientation in day-to-day life can view their dreams as a self-fulfilling prophecy. For example, a dream about not performing well in a job interview—you'll be either too stressed to showcase your best skills or less motivated to prepare well for the interview.

Theories about Dream Symbolism

Dream interpretation plays a crucial role in psychoanalysis. Due to this, several analysts have developed theories about dreams and their meanings. Sigmund Freud and Carl Jung were two leading psychoanalysts who found dream images compelling to analyze and use as therapeutic tools.

At the beginning of the twentieth century, most scientists were not concerned about attaching too many meanings to people's dreams. Most of them assumed that dream images were by-products of the brain processing information during the REM phase of sleep. Some scientists even support this theory today, and non-professionals guided by their theories often dismiss unfavorable dream events. After all, how many times have you heard someone describing their bad dream images as silly dreams? Freud, on the other hand, noticed early on that his patients' dreams were meaningful—regardless of how little a person remembered from their dreams or how little their dream images meant to the particular person.

Freud affirmed that with research, professionals could develop procedures for successful dream interpretation. He began by laying the foundation with his dream interpretation theory. He found that the key to interpreting dreams more effectively was simply letting the person describe whatever details they could remember. This prompted people to follow their trains of thought rather than being influenced by how the professional interprets them. They could form their own ideas of what their dreams could have meant.

By practicing free association (between dream images and the thoughts they evoke), Freud found that there were four elements in dream work. The first one is condensation. It is referred to as the piling up of several ideas in one dream—as the information of all these ideas was pulled into one thought and shown as one dream picture. The second element is displacement, which is associated with hidden emotional meanings. This often happens when the dreamer confuses significant and meaningless parts of their dreams. The third is symbolization, which points to repressed ideas only shown as items that symbolize their meaning. Secondary revision is the fourth element. It denotes the reorganization of dreams, which makes them easier to understand and remember.

Most people focus on what they can consciously remember from their dreams. However, as Freud—and later Jung—agreed, dreams are more of a sorting process for the brain for all daytime experiences. This affects how the brain functions and why it hides some parts of the dream world in the subconscious. People's brains are constantly changing due to their subconscious content, evolving to accommodate the type of information the brain gathers and processes. Mentored by Freud, Jung also found allies in dreams when treating mental conditions. Freud and Jung brought more in-depth insights into dream interpretation from the science of their era and other ancient sources, including history, mythology, and art. Their work helped them amass significant knowledge about the human psyche.

This, in turn, enabled the next generation of dream interpreters and psychoanalysts to understand the nature of dreams and how they interact with the body and mind.

Their agreement and cooperation notwithstanding, there were fundamental differences between Jung's and Freud's theories about dream interpretation. Whereas his mentor looked into the past causes of dreams, Jung's work was focused on the future implication of dreams. He considered dream images critical to reveal information about the patient's health development in the future. He established several functions for the dreams. The primary was compensation—which he called the brain's way of maintaining the balance between conscious and subconscious ideas. According to Jung, if a conscious person tries to repress their subconscious thoughts, their dreams will show the imbalance and prompt them to return to their balanced self.

The second function of dreams—according to Jung—is reductive compensation. This is a unique form of Jung's compensation. It's a more severe attempt from one's dreams to reinstate the balance lost due to the inflated conscious ego that tries to control everything in waking life. Jung believed that dreams can always tell a person who they are and who they have the potential to be. If you have an opinion about yourself that does not reflect reality, the dreams will have you face the truth. They will compensate for your mistaken beliefs by showing you images that contradict your ideas about yourself. They bring you back into the depths of your psyche, allowing you to develop a more accurate self-picture. For example, if you think your actions always reflect great morals—even if they do not—your dreams will likely remind you of all your thoughts, emotions, and actions that point to faulty morals.

The prospective function of a dream is yet another one determined by Jung. While he believed most dreams could fulfill the first two functions, he didn't exclude the possibility of dream images having other purposes. He proposed a third fundamental function of dreams: The prospective function. This is very similar to the prophetic ideas traditional religious systems have about dreams. Prospective dreams offer glimpses into potential future events. According to Jung, the role of this function is to help a person's growth and guide them on their path toward achieving integration and balance. If people can learn to interpret these prophetic dreams, they can access a unique pool of wisdom hidden in their subconscious minds.

Types of Dreams

While it is still unclear how many dreams people can have, there is a universal estimation of the number. Below are the most common dream types.

Daydreams

Most people would describe daydreaming as having vivid visions during waking hours. These visions are associated with hidden desires, fantasies, or unfulfilled expectations. At other times, they may be desired outcomes of potential situations or reveries of past occurrences. Daydreams are more common than you think. They are also more easily remembered than the dreams from sleeping hours—although most people dismiss them faster than any other type of dream.

Epic Dreams

These dreams are vivid dreams that, true to their names, are too epic to forget. They are one of the most interpreted dream forms, even though it takes some work to pin down their meaning. Interpreters consider these as profound experiences with long-standing effects and, depending on whether you adhere to their message, have the potential to change your life. The condition called epic dream disorder causes people to have these memorable dreams in their sleep without any emotional meaning. These excessive dreams typically involve people doing day-to-day tasks in their dreams until they become so tired that they wake up exhausted in the morning.

False Awakening Dreams

Some people go through their morning routine in their dream thinking they are already awake—when, in fact, they're still profoundly asleep. This is called a false awakening, resulting from a transition from REM sleep to the light sleep phase. REM sleep is responsible for mental health recovery, so these dreams are a way of your mind preparing you mentally for the day ahead. False awakenings are linked to lucid dreams.

Nightmares

People abruptly wake up from sleep due to their overwhelming effect.[1]

Nightmares are described as disturbing or downright frightening dreams showcasing images laced with negative emotions, like despair, fear, disgust, sadness, or a combination of these emotions. Due to their overwhelming effect, nightmares cause most people to wake up suddenly. However, they may typically dismiss it as a normal occurrence. In rare cases, nightmares become so intense that they disturb a person's sleep and waking life. Commonly occurring vivid nightmares can have a detrimental effect on your cognitive functions.

Night Terrors

Night terrors are similar to nightmares, except they're accompanied by sounds and movements a person makes while sleeping. They're the most common in older children and adolescents; however, a small percentage of adults also have them regularly. Some night terrors involve a person making only a few movements and sounds. Others cause them to scream and flail for several minutes or even longer.

Progressive Dreams

Due to their unique nature, progressive dreams are still uncharted territory. Interpreters define them as a sequence of images with a continuous narrative. Essentially, you are experiencing a story unfolding as you keep dreaming about the same thing. The dreams can follow each other nightly, like continuously reading a book or sporadically watching a new series on TV and waiting for the still-to-come episodes.

Lucid Dreams

Lucid dreams are rarely recorded. They involve a person being suspended between the dream state and conscious wakefulness. Interestingly enough, some people retain the awareness and the ability to control their dream. Others can even communicate consciously in lucid dreams. Dream interpreters suggest that, through practice and discipline, it is possible to train yourself to have a lucid dream.

Prophetic Dreams

Prophetic dreams have brought the fascination of dream interpretation into people's lives. For centuries, people have believed dreams can predict the future. Some people are inclined to prophetic dreams and can analyze and interpret them effortlessly. They can use precognition for guidance, healing, warning, and other purposes to manifest more detailed outcomes.

Recurring Dreams

Recurring dreams are the replay of the same dream images. They often reflect an unresolved issue, unmet desire, or the brain's struggle to process traumatic experiences during waking hours. Sometimes recurring dreams only involve one particular image, whereas, on other occasions, you will see the repeat of an entire dream sequence. The dreams can continue until the cause is resolved or replaced with something else.

Vivid Dreams

Vivid dreams are caused by a condition called REM rebound, which is related to mental health recovery. This is your mind's way of compensating for being sleep-deprived because of stress or other factors. During REM, you experience heightened brain activity, which creates vivid dreams. These dreams are also common when people have a high fever, which hinders the brain's ability to regulate its activity during sleep.

The Benefits of Dream Interpretation

Learning to analyze and comprehend your dreams takes some time and practice. As you embark on this journey, you will notice that while some dream images can be discerned effortlessly, most will be far more complex. Whether you rely only on your intuition or use the help of known dream symbols will be up to you. However, it will be easier to help you get started if you know the benefits of dream interpretation.

Here are see several advantages of dream work to inspire you to commence this journey:

- Dreams can help you find yourself. If you are struggling to find your path, your dreams can steer you in the right direction.
- Dreams can help you stay healthy. By warning you about future health, your dreams can help you prevent illnesses by seeking help and adopting a healthier lifestyle.
- Dreams can keep you safe. Many people receive warnings about environmental events in dreams, which help them escape dangerous situations.
- Dreams will not let you deny the truth. They show you an issue as it is, enabling you to learn the truth of every situation. While sobering, a healthy dose of dream reality is necessary for a happy life.
- Dreams can provide solutions for real-life issues. Sometimes, the only way your mind can work through a problem is to pull out a solution from the subconscious and show it to you in your dreams.
- Dreams show how you feel about people, events, and situations. If you have any pent-up feelings you leave to fester in your waking life, dreams can help release them, preventing them from causing further disturbances in your life and health.
- Dreams help build better relationships. Your dreams can warn you about red flags in a relationship you would otherwise ignore due to emotional involvement. They can help you eliminate toxic people from your life, so you can focus on building a connection with people who contribute positively to your life. Dreams can also help you identify the right romantic partner, the best ways to resolve issues in your relationships, build harmony, and keep your love life enjoyable for you and your partner.
- Dreams can help you communicate with your ancestors. Departed loved ones can visit you in your dreams, leaving you messages—but you'll only know they have done this if you take your time to learn dream interpretation. This ancient art will help

you reveal the difference between spiritual messages and messages coming from your subconscious.
- Dreams will show you your future. They can help you glimpse into future outcomes based on current actions. This lets you decide whether to continue on your current path or change course to get a different outcome.
- Dreams are the key to spiritual and mental growth. The messages you receive in your dreams can reflect the information you need to become a better person or obtain the spiritual enlightenment you desire.
- Dreams offer peace of mind. If nothing else, interpreting your dreams will have a therapeutic effect on your mental health. By showing you what your conscious mind struggles with, you're gaining an insight into the causation of your symptoms. After learning where they come from, it will be much easier to chase away anxiety and other symptoms.

Chapter 2: Remember Your Dreams and Look for Patterns

Dreams can be mysterious, fascinating, and sometimes even terrifying. They can bring you to unknown places, introduce unfamiliar faces, and present bizarre scenarios that often leave you wondering what they mean. They have been the topic of numerous discussions, debates, and interpretations across different cultures and civilizations. However, one of the biggest challenges that people face when trying to interpret their dreams is remembering them.

How often have you woken up in the morning, unable to recall a single detail of what you dreamed the night before? The frustrating feeling of knowing that you had a dream but not being able to remember it can be quite common. But why does this happen? The science behind why people struggle to remember their dreams still needs to be fully understood. However, it has something to do with the fact that dreams occur during the Rapid Eye Movement (REM) stage of sleep, which is the deepest stage, so it is even more challenging to remember the details of your dreams.

Despite these challenges, remembering your dreams can be incredibly helpful in gaining insight into your subconscious mind. By paying attention to recurring themes, symbols, and emotions in your dreams, you can unravel their meaning and better understand your inner self. This chapter will provide various techniques to help you improve your dream recall, like keeping a dream journal and creating a bedtime routine.

Why You Have Trouble Remembering Dreams

During a typical sleep cycle, the brain goes through several stages of sleep. These stages are categorized into two main types: Non-Rapid Eye Movement (NREM) sleep and Rapid Eye Movement (REM) sleep. NREM sleep has three stages, while REM sleep constitutes only one stage. REM sleep is known as the deepest stage of sleep, as it is associated with a high level of brain activity and increased physiological responses. During this time, the brain becomes more active, and the body experiences changes in heart rate, blood pressure, and respiration. It is also during this stage that people have most of their dreams.

Although REM sleep is a vital part of the sleep cycle, it's challenging to remember your dreams. The brain is more active during REM sleep, and the body is in a state of deep relaxation, making it more difficult to recall the details of the dream. Additionally, REM sleep occurs toward the end of the sleep cycle, which means that when you wake up, you are more likely to remember the dreams you had earlier in the night, during the lighter stages of sleep, than those that occurred during the REM stage. Furthermore, the brain processes and stores memories during sleep; however, this can be interrupted by the REM stage, leading to difficulty with recall. The memories formed during REM sleep may be more challenging to retrieve as the brain is more active, and there is a higher level of neural activity, making it harder to separate memories from dreams.

Techniques to Enhance Your Sleep Recall

Sleep recall, or the ability to remember your dreams, can be an elusive phenomenon for many people. However, with a few simple techniques, you can improve your recall and unlock the hidden world of your dreams. Here are some techniques to help you improve your sleep recall:

1. Keep a Dream Journal

Keeping a dream journal will train your brain to remember your dreams more vividly.[2]

Keep a notebook near your bed and write down your dreams as soon as you wake up. This practice can help you train your brain to remember your dreams more vividly. Dream journaling can include these steps:

Step 1: Choose a Journal

Choosing a dedicated journal for your dreams helps you stay organized and consistent. You can use a physical journal or an app on your phone or computer. Choose one that you like and find easy to use. Consider using a hardcover journal or one with sturdy binding that can withstand frequent use. Plus, you can decorate your journal to make the process more appealing.

Step 2: Record the Dream

Start each dream entry with the date, including the day of the week. This helps you track your dreams and identify patterns. Write down everything you remember about the dream, including colors, emotions, people, and events. Be as specific and detailed as possible, using descriptive language. This can help you capture the essence of the dream and remember it more vividly. Try to write down the dream as soon as you wake up—before getting out of bed or doing anything else. This will help you remember more details.

Step 3: Underline Key Elements

As you write, underline or highlight the main themes, recurring objects, or people in your dreams. This will give insight into your subconscious mind. For example, if you often dream about flying, underline "flying" or "wings" in your dream entries. You can use a different color pen or highlighter to underline key elements. This makes them stand out and easier to find later.

Step 4: Add Context

If possible, write down any context relevant to the dream, such as your mood before going to bed or any events that happened during the day. This can help you understand why you had the dream and what it may mean. Use abbreviations or shorthand for context information to save time and space. For example, you could use "Mood: Anxious" or "Event: Meeting with boss."

Step 5: Reflect on the Dream

After recording the dream, take a moment to reflect on its meaning or any insights it might offer. You can also write down any questions you have about the dream. This can help you understand the dream on a deeper level and uncover its underlying messages. Write down your initial reactions and feelings about the dream, and capture your initial impressions and insights.

Step 6: Repeat

Make a habit of recording your dreams every morning, even if you do not remember much at first. Over time, this practice will help you train your brain to remember details and dreams more easily. Set aside a specific time each morning to record your dreams, such as right after waking up or during your morning routine. This can help you establish a consistent habit. Consider using a reward system to motivate yourself to record your dreams regularly. For example, you could reward yourself with a small treat or activity each time you record a dream for a certain number of days in a row.

2. Use the 5Ws Technique

The 5Ws method is a simplified approach to dream recall that focuses on answering the five basic questions: Who? What? When? Where? and why? It is a great option for people who have less time to keep a detailed dream journal.

Step 1: Write Down the Five Questions

On a piece of paper or your digital format, write down the five questions: Who? What? When? Where? and Why? Leave enough space under each question to write your answers. Use a consistent format for the questions, such as all caps or bold text, to make them stand out.

Step 2: Recall the Dream

Think back to your dream and try to remember as many details as possible. Focus on answering the five questions with as much information as you can recall.

Step 3: Answer the Questions

Under each question, write down your answers. Be as specific using descriptive language.

- Who? Write down any people or characters who appeared in the dream, including yourself and others.
- What? Write down any events, actions, or objects that appeared in the dream.
- When? Write down any time-related details, such as the time of day or how much time seemed to pass in the dream.
- Where? Write down any locations or settings that appeared in the dream, including any changes in location.
- Why? Write down any emotions, motivations, or reasons that might have contributed to the dream.

If you cannot remember an answer to a question, leave it blank and move on. You can always come back to it later if you remember more details.

3. Practice Lucid Dreaming

Lucid dreaming is the ability to control your dreams consciously. By practicing lucid dreaming, you can become more aware of your dreams, making it easier to remember them later.

Step 1: Set Your Intention

Before you go to bed, set your intention to have a lucid dream. Repeat affirmations like "*I will become aware that I am dreaming*" or "*I will have a lucid dream tonight*" to help your subconscious mind prepare for the experience.

Step 2: Reality Checks

Throughout the day, take reality checks to increase your awareness of whether you are dreaming. Ask yourself questions like *"Am I dreaming right now?"* and perform actions like looking at your hands, which can appear distorted or unusual in dreams.

Step 3: Induce Lucid Dreaming

There are several techniques you can use to induce lucid dreaming. Some popular methods include:

- <u>Wake-Back-to-Bed (WBTB) Technique:</u> Set an alarm to wake up after five or six hours of sleep and stay awake for thirty to 60 minutes before returning to bed. This technique increases your chances of having a lucid dream.
- <u>Mnemonic Induction of Lucid Dreams (MILD) Technique:</u> Before going to sleep, repeat a phrase like *"I will have a lucid dream tonight"* while visualizing yourself becoming lucid in a dream. This technique programs your subconscious to induce lucid dreaming.
- <u>Wake-Initiated Lucid Dream (WILD) Technique:</u> This involves staying awake while your body falls asleep. Lie down in a comfortable position and focus on your breathing or a simple mental image. As your body falls asleep, you may enter a lucid dream.

Step 4: Stay Calm and Engage with the Dream

Once you realize you're in a lucid dream, stay calm and engage with the dream. You can try different things like flying, talking to dream characters, or exploring your dream world. The more you engage with the dream, the longer you will stay in a lucid state.

Step 5: Exit the Dream

When you're ready to wake up, try to exit the dream gently. You can try closing your eyes and imagining yourself waking up in bed or simply letting the dream fade away.

4. Create a Dream Map

Create a visual map of your dreams using images, symbols, and colors. This can help you remember your dreams more vividly and connect with their emotions and themes.

Step 1: Gather Your Materials

Collect art supplies like colored pencils, markers, and paper. You can also add images from magazines or printouts from the internet to your map.

Step 2: Set the Scene

Start by drawing a landscape or setting that represents your dream world. This can be a cityscape, forest, or any other environment you recall from your dreams.

Step 3: Add Symbols and Images

Think about the characters, objects, and events that appeared in your dream and draw or cut out images that represent them. Use symbols and colors that feel meaningful, even if they do not match the objects exactly.

Step 4: Connect the Dots

As you add more symbols and images to your map, look for connections between them. Are there recurring themes or emotions? Are certain objects or characters always present together? Draw lines or arrows to connect these elements.

Step 5: Reflect on Your Map

Once you have finished your dream map, reflect on what you've created for a few moments. What themes or emotions are present? Are there any surprises or insights that you gained from the process?

Step 6: Use Your Dream Map

Keep your dream map in a visible place where you can see it regularly, like on your bedroom wall or in your journal. Use it as a tool for dream recall and reflection, and add to it as you have new dreams. The more you engage with your dream map, the more vivid and meaningful your dreams may become.

5. Visualize Your Dreams

Use guided visualization techniques to help you remember and explore your dreams in more detail. Imagine yourself back in the dream, and ask yourself questions about what you experienced. This can help you unlock hidden meanings and insights from your dreams.

Step 1: Relax Your Mind and Body

Find a quiet, comfortable place where you will not be disturbed. Close your eyes, take a few deep breaths, and allow your body to relax. You can also listen to calming music or guided meditation recordings to help you relax.

Step 2: Recall Your Dream

Think back to a recent dream that you want to explore further. Remember as many details as possible, including the setting, characters, and events.

Step 3: Visualize Yourself in the Dream

Imagine yourself back in the dream as if you were watching it unfold before your eyes. Visualize the setting and characters as vividly as you can. Try to engage all your senses, noticing any sounds, smells, or textures you can recall.

Step 4: Ask Questions

As you visualize yourself in the dream, ask yourself questions about what you are experiencing. For example, you could ask, "What does this character represent?" or "What is the significance of this object?" Use your intuition and imagination to explore different interpretations and meanings.

Step 5: Reflect on Your Insights

After you have spent some time exploring your dream through visualization, take a few moments to reflect on any insights or revelations that you gained. Write them down in a dream journal, along with any lingering questions or mysteries.

6. Use Dream Art

Create art inspired by your dreams, such as paintings, drawings, or collages. This helps you to connect with the emotions and themes of your dreams and bring them to life in a tangible way.

Painting or drawing your expression of what you dream about can be therapeutic.[8]

Step 1: Set Up Your Art Supplies

Gather your art supplies, such as pencils, markers, watercolors, or digital tools. Have a sketchbook or piece of paper ready to work on.

Step 2: Think about Your Dream

Take a moment to focus on the dream you want to remember. What images or symbols stand out? What colors or emotions are associated with the dream? You can also look at any notes or journals you have kept about the dream.

Step 3: Start Creating

Use your art supplies to create a visual representation of your dream. This can be a realistic drawing, an abstract painting, or even a collage of images and symbols. Focus on capturing the essence of the dream rather than trying to recreate it exactly.

Step 4: Add Details and Descriptions

As you work on your dream art, write down any details or descriptions that come to mind. This helps you remember the dream more clearly and make connections between different elements.

Step 5: Reflect on Your Dream Art

Take some time to reflect on the dream art you've created. What emotions or insights does it bring up? Are there any patterns or themes that emerge? Write down any thoughts or reflections in your dream journal.

7. Dream Sharing

Before bed, focus on specific dream cues or triggers, such as a recurring dream symbol or a particular emotion. This can increase your chances of recognizing these cues in your dreams and help you remember more details.

Step 1: Choose a Trusted Friend or Family Member

You want to make sure that you feel comfortable being vulnerable with them and that they will provide positive feedback and support.

Step 2: Set Aside Time

Set aside time to talk about your dreams regularly. This could be once a week or every few weeks, depending on your schedule and availability. Find a time that works for both you and your dream-sharing partner.

Step 3: Recollect Your Dreams

Before your scheduled time to share, ensure you clearly recollect your dreams. Keep your dream journal beside your bed and write down as many details as you can remember upon waking up.

Step 4: Share

When it is time to share, start by giving an overview of the dream, including any emotions, themes, or important details that stood out to you. Be descriptive and use specific language.

Step 5: Get Insight

Listen to your dream-sharing partner's feedback and insights. Ask questions and clarify any points that are not clear. Be open to different perspectives and interpretations of your dreams.

Remembering your dreams can be a valuable tool for personal growth, self-discovery, and creativity. Dreams can provide insights into your subconscious mind and offer solutions to problems you may be struggling with in your waking life. By making a conscious effort to remember and analyze dreams, you can gain a deeper understanding of yourself and the world around you. In addition to the mentioned techniques, relaxation exercises such as meditation or deep breathing can quieten the mind and promote a deeper sleep, resulting in more vivid dreams.

It's also important to note that not all dreams hold significant meanings or symbolism. Some dreams may simply reflect your daily experiences or result from random neural firings during sleep. Therefore, it's essential to approach dream interpretation with an open mind and not get too caught up in trying to find meaning in every dream. It's also worth mentioning that everyone's dreams are unique to them. Personal experiences, cultural background, and individual beliefs can influence dreams. Therefore, while there may be some universal symbols and archetypes, it's crucial to remember that the interpretation of a dream is ultimately up to the dreamer.

Chapter 3: What Are You Doing in Your Dream?

Dreams often mimic real life. Everything you see and experience in your waking life can find its way into your dreams. When you close your eyes to sleep at night, you usually see yourself doing activities like running, eating, or laughing, while in other dreams, you see some of your worst fears realized, like falling from the sky or drowning. However, with dreams, everything has a different meaning.

This chapter will discuss everyday actions and activities you see in your dreams and what they symbolize.

Drowning

Drowning is one of the worst nightmares, yet has positive and negative meanings. It can indicate that you are overwhelmed in your waking life and need a break. The dream can also mean that you are under a lot of stress and feel like you are drowning and need to catch your breath. Since water is associated with rebirth, it can symbolize renewal, new beginnings, and transformation.

Dreaming of drowning can have negative and positive interpretations.[4]

Avoiding Drowning

If you save yourself from drowning, it indicates you can avoid harmful situations that can impact your spiritual, physical, and mental well-being. Even if you face challenges and obstacles, you will overcome them and come out stronger. It also means that good luck is coming your way, so you should be prepared.

Dying by Drowning

If you drown and die in your dream, it is a sign that you are unable to cope with your inhibitions and emotions. Thus, you need to change your mindset and start adopting a positive attitude toward your life.

Drowning in a Swimming Boat

Since pools are human-made, dreaming that you are drowning in one indicates that someone in your circle is causing you trouble or that you are the one making things hard for yourself. You have probably set unattainable goals for yourself and cannot accomplish them. It can also mean a close friend you trust is causing your problems. They could be jealous and spiteful and have no problem betraying you.

Drowning on a Boat

In dreams, boats symbolize the course you are taking in your life. If you dream you are on a sinking boat, you are about to face challenges in your waking life. You are under a lot of stress, and this dream is telling you to slow down. You are probably feeling exhausted in your waking life or feel anxious about your life at the moment. If you are steering the boat while it is sinking, nothing is going right in your life.

Seeing a Loved One Drowning

Dreaming of a loved one drowning suggests you are afraid to lose them. You are worried about someone in your life who could be dying or struggling with health issues.

Seeing Yourself Drowning

If you are the one drowning, you are experiencing negative emotions in real life, like anxiety, fear, or depression. You feel that you are making yourself miserable and can do nothing to change your situation.

Eating

Eating dreams are usually pleasant unless you are eating something inedible. This dream could simply mean that you went to bed hungry or are on a diet and craving a certain type of food, like pizza or chocolate. However, this dream can have other different meanings. It is not just the act of eating; the food and taste can also have meanings. If the food tastes strange, you missed a big opportunity in your waking life. Experiencing the food's texture, sensation, and taste in the dream means you are ambitious and driven to succeed.

Eating can symbolize a hunger for something missing in your life, like love, recognition, or a better career. It can suggest there is a goal you want or are excited about and cannot wait to accomplish, like buying a new car or losing weight. How you eat your food in your dream represents how much you want to achieve this goal.

Eating Alone

Dreaming about eating alone can signify several things.[5]

Eating alone in your dream indicates you feel lost or isolated from the people in your life. However, if you feel happy or relaxed during your meal, you require some peace and quiet in your waking life.

If you are unhappy while eating alone in your dream, you feel lonely and should do something to conquer this feeling.

Eating Something Inedible

Not all eating dreams are about food. Eating something inedible means that you do not know how to deal with the problems in your life, and you need to confront them right away.

Eating with Others

Eating with other people in your dreams has a more positive meaning than eating alone. It shows your comfort in social situations and that you have a great relationship with the people in your life. It can also mean you desire to connect with others or lack friendships.

Lack of Food

Lack of food or not having enough food in your dream indicates that something is missing in your life. You can also be hungry for new experiences. You are doing something in your life that does not bring you any satisfaction, or you have achieved a goal you have been working on for a long time, but you still feel unhappy.

Overeating

Overeating in your dream means you are overwhelmed in your waking life. You are under a lot of stress, and you need a break. It can also indicate that you're feeling insecure and need to impress someone or are trying to get a person you are interested in to notice you. The dream can also signify that you need a change in your life.

Poisonous Food

Poisonous food means you're struggling with a problem in your waking life. Someone close to you has disappointed you, or a job or experience you had high hopes for made you miserable. It can also mean you're working hard to achieve a goal but are nowhere near accomplishing it and feel hopeless.

Falling

Falling dreams are common and unpleasant, and they usually have different meanings. They can symbolize a lack of control over various issues in your life, which lead to anxiety, fear, and helplessness. Interpreting this dream depends on finding clues within the context of your dream.

Falling dreams are one of the most common.[6]

Dreaming of Someone Else Falling

This dream means you are worried about losing someone you care about, like your partner leaving you. It also indicates that a loved one is struggling with control in their life, and you're worried about them.

Falling Down an Elevator

Dreaming you are falling down an elevator or stairs symbolizes poor emotional well-being and low self-confidence. You could also be worried that things are changing around you and you cannot keep up with others. This dream also means that you're emotionally hurt. If you manage to get out of the elevator or someone saves you, new opportunities are coming your way.

Falling into the Darkness

Falling into an unknown place or a dark abyss means that you are afraid of something in real life. Your dream is telling you to confront these fears right away. If this is a recurrent dream, see what clues or messages it is giving you and re-evaluate your life to see what you need to address. Fear of the unknown and the future is usually the main trigger behind this dream.

Getting Hurt

Dreaming that you fell and got hurt means you are unable to confront certain aspects of yourself and your life, like failing to achieve your goals or living up to your expectations. It can also indicate that you can't overcome certain challenges alone.

Seeing Yourself Falling

If you are the one falling into your dream, you feel rejected, anxious, insecure, overwhelmed, inferior, helpless, and out of control. Seeing someone pushing you off a cliff means that you feel insecure in your life. You suffer from low self-esteem if you trip and fall from a cliff. In all contexts, you do not feel in control of your life. Falling from a plane while wearing a parachute indicates freedom and letting go of whatever is holding you back.

Tripping and Falling

If you can't see what you tripped over, it means someone in your life is getting on your nerves. If you trip on a banana or any other object, you need to take care of yourself and the people in your life. The dream can also have a positive meaning, like getting an unexpected and happy surprise.

Flying

Flying can be a pleasant or terrifying dream, depending on the context. It can mean feeling free and that everything is possible. You can go anywhere, do anything, and be anyone. It shows you can handle anything life throws your way.

The negative meaning behind this dream reflects that there is something in your life you cannot live with and are trying to escape from. Sometimes, this dream means you are stressed in your waking life.

Flying a Plane

Flying in your dream symbolizes that you are in control of your life and where you are heading. Planes take you from one destination to another, so the dream can indicate that you are going to another place or starting a new chapter in your life. If the plane crashes or you experience turbulence, you will face obstacles on your way.

Falling Down

If you are flying and suddenly see yourself falling, it means you're struggling with personal growth and self-improvement. You can have obstacles in your life that prevent you from advancing, and you need to overcome them.

Fear of Flying

Feeling afraid while flying suggests you are a negative thinker. These thoughts are preventing you from enjoying your life and everything it has to offer. It can also mean that you're attached to your past, have a need to always be in control, or your goals are hard to achieve.

Flying High

Flying high in your dream represents freedom, lack of obstacles, and success. You have overcome some challenges in your waking life, like getting a promotion you worked hard for or achieving financial success. However, this dream can also have a different meaning. You can constantly brag about yourself in front of others, and your subconscious tells you to be more down to earth.

Flying with Wings

If you dream that you have wings and fly like a bird, it indicates you are free-spirited or experiencing new beginnings and feeling hopeful. It can also mean great opportunities are coming your way and will bring you joy and happiness. The dream can symbolize feeling empowered and strong.

You have succeeded in getting rid of everything that holds you back, and you feel invincible.

Struggling to Fly

Dreaming that you are struggling to fly or unable to stay in the air for more than a few seconds suggests that something in your life is preventing you from improving or advancing. It is trying to tell you where the problem lies, so pay attention to the context of your dream; it can provide you with clues.

Laughing

Laughing is always pleasant, but just like anything in the dream world, it can have positive and negative meanings. If your laugh is natural and not hysterical, it means that you are happy and satisfied in your waking life. Laughing can also mean you're overwhelmed with tension and stress, and you need to take care of yourself and have fun. The dream also represents your satisfaction with your life. Most people wake up smiling when they are laughing in their dream.

Laughing and Crying

Dreaming that you are laughing and crying at the same time indicates confusion. You have probably experienced difficult situations in the last few months, feel sensitive, and struggle to cope. Whenever you try to stay positive, you find yourself pulled back into a circle of darkness and negativity. No one can help you but you.

Laughing Loudly

This dream means you enjoy being the center of attention. You want all eyes to be on you, and you always try to get a reaction from others. There is something about you that makes people enjoy your company and laugh wherever you are around. You desire to be liked, which drives you crazy when someone dislikes you.

Laughing Quietly

Laughing quietly in a dream reflects your patience. You are calm and poised, and do not let stress get to you. No matter what the situation, you never react with anger or aggression.

Someone Else Laughing

Dreaming of someone laughing means that you will have happy experiences soon. You may go on a vacation with your friends or a loved one, or you will celebrate good news soon. The dream can also foretell that something you're waiting for will finally happen, like getting married, having a baby, or getting a promotion.

Someone Laughing at You

Dreaming of someone laughing at you means that something in your life requires attention, and you should force yourself to handle the situation. It can also indicate that you have a strong personality. This dream can also be a warning that you are about to receive bad news or are surrounded by negative energy.

Uncontrollable Laughter

This dream reflects your out-of-control emotions. You easily lose your temper and react without thinking. It is telling you to stop overreacting to every situation and think before speaking.

Running

Running is one of the most recurring dreams. It is not usually a pleasant dream since you either escape from something or chase someone. Generally, running means escaping reality, personal growth, getting away from your problems, overcoming challenges, and, in some cases, experiencing joy. If you are running fast and hard, you should find a goal in your life to run toward.

Running slowly means you will struggle with achieving your goals in real life. You could also be running to avoid something or someone in your real life, like a work task, an exam, or relationship issues. When you are running from or toward something, you feel anxious or guilty about an issue in your waking life. Running without a purpose indicates worry and anxiety about your future or feeling trapped or struggling with making a decision.

Running Away from Someone

Dreaming that you are running away from someone or something means that you're trying to avoid or escape from your fears. You feel in danger or threatened, so you flee. Sometimes, you can be running from something inside of you, like your impulses or inner struggles. Seeing the face of the person or thing chasing you can give you an insight into what is troubling you.

Running for Exercise

Dreaming that you are running for exercise represents working to improve yourself and your life. However, the dream can also indicate that you're wasting your effort on the wrong things, like a project or a career. Analyze and research the issue carefully before taking any steps.

Running in Fear

If you are running to save yourself from someone chasing you and are scared, you feel protected and safe in your surroundings. You can also be heading on a dangerous path, and this dream serves as a warning to have your guard up. This dream can also reflect certain issues you're struggling with in your waking life.

Running to Hide

If you dream you are running to hide, you should look at yourself and re-evaluate your life. You can be under a lot of stress and need to slow down, or things are changing around you, and you do not feel in control. This dream also symbolizes avoidance. There is an issue in your life you cannot confront, like a secret or a sad memory you're trying to block.

Running toward Someone

Running toward someone in your dreams has two meanings. It can indicate that you are working on a difficult goal but far from accomplishing it. In this case, evaluate your strategies to determine what needs change. It can also reflect your ambition and desire to achieve your goals immediately. You're on the right track, and you can achieve anything you set your mind to and turn your dream into a reality.

Unable to Run

Dreaming that you are trying to run but cannot move your feet is a recurring dream, usually resulting from REM paralysis. However, it can reflect that you're suffering from poor self-esteem.

In the land of dreams, nothing is as it seems. Drowning can have a positive meaning, while laughter can have a negative one. Pay attention to your dreams and understand the meaning behind everything you see. Your subconscious is painting you a picture, and every detail matters.

Chapter 4: Dream Locations and Meanings

Dreams take place in settings that are real or imaginary. More often than not, they change during the dream, while at other times, you do not even notice the location as the events take precedence. When people interpret their dreams, they are usually more focused on the scenario than where it occurred. However, similar to actions, your subconscious is also trying to tell you something through the location of your dreams.

Dreamworlds reflect your mindset. They don't symbolize a place but what you think of in your waking life. For instance, dreaming about your office means you're preoccupied with your job. If you dream about returning to school, you're concerned about the life lessons you hope to learn. Dreaming about your childhood home suggests you're still attached to the past. Once you understand the meaning behind different common locations, you will better understand yourself.

This chapter will cover different dream locations and the meanings and symbolism behind them.

Amusement Park

Dreaming of an amusement park symbolizes your need to take a break and have fun. Perhaps you have been working too hard and need more time for yourself. It can also indicate feeling nostalgic for your carefree childhood. The dream could further reflect your desire to escape reality, even temporarily.

Dreaming about an amusement park symbolizes the need for a break.⁷

If you are not enjoying yourself in the park, you feel trapped and do not have any control over your life.

Crowded Amusement Park

Dreaming of a crowded amusement park reflects your fear of loneliness. You need the love and support of your family and friends to combat this feeling. It can also mean you are struggling with making a decision. Many people try to influence your opinion, and you cannot think clearly.

Roller Coaster

A roller coaster in dreams indicates that you don't take anything seriously. It means you are trying to better your life and take it one day at a time. Riding a roller coaster with a loved one symbolizes the highs and lows of your relationship. It represents your desire to have new and fun experiences with them. The roller coaster can also symbolize that your relationship with this person will change or external factors will impact both of you. These changes will be positive if you're having fun on the ride. However, if you feel scared or uncomfortable, they will be unpleasant. If you aren't enjoying the ride in the dream, you'll not embrace the changes in your waking life.

Beach

Seeing the beach in your dreams suggests reflecting on yourself and your life. You are about to undergo big changes that can be good or bad, like a marriage proposal or a breakup. It also means that you are at peace with whatever happens in your life. You have decided to look on the bright side and accept anything that happens to you with a smile and gratitude. This dream suggests you are about to go on a vacation that will be a much-needed escape so you can recharge and refocus on your goals.

Empty or Deserted Beach

This dream means you feel empty on the inside. Your subconscious is telling you to look inward to find yourself and fill the emptiness. Forget about what you have to do and focus on the things that bring you joy. This dream can also symbolize transition.

A deserted beach means you are exhausted and desperately need a break. You want to be in a place with nothing and no one to worry about but yourself.

Sunbathing on the Beach

This dream symbolizes nostalgia and returning to a time when you were carefree and at peace. It also means you long to experience something new and amazing.

Childhood Home

Dreaming about your childhood signifies feeling nostalgic for the past. You probably feel unsupported and unloved by the people in your life and are looking for the comfort of your childhood. Or simply, your brain is trying to escape the unpleasantness of your waking life to a safe and happy memory. It can also mean that you long for a time when life was simple. Sometimes, the past can bring bad memories and resentment, and your subconscious is telling you that it is time to confront it and let go of the anger and the pain.

Better Childhood Home

Dreaming of a better and bigger childhood home suggests that the principles and ideals you have grown up with have positively impacted your life. Your happy childhood has influenced the strong and successful person you have become.

Destroyed Childhood Home

Dreaming of your childhood home being destroyed suggests unpleasant memories are haunting you. It can also mean that an old secret you have kept all your life has now come to light. Perhaps you have created a false childhood image, and the truth is now being revealed.

Church or Temple

Seeing a place of worship in your dream, like a church or temple, indicates your need for support and guidance from a god or higher place. It also means two choices confront you, and you do not know which is right for you. You are also struggling with existential questions like "Why are you here?" or "What does the future hold?" Houses of worship in dreams can reflect your desire to connect with your spiritual side.

Being in a Church or Temple

If you are struggling with hardships in your waking life, this dream represents your frustration and confusion over what to do in this situation. You are desperate, feel there is no way out, and are about to give up on your goals. Your self-esteem is shaking, and you no longer have faith in your abilities. The houses of worship symbolize your faith. Being in a church or temple in your dream is a sign that you can overcome these obstacles.

Closed Church or Temple

Seeing a closed church or temple in your dream means you feel helpless and alone. Perhaps a close friend or a family member has recently disappointed you. Your subconscious is telling you to take the high road and open your heart to forgiveness.

City

A city in dreams symbolizes a fast-paced and lively lifestyle. It can indicate that your life is changing at a pace you are uncomfortable with, and you struggle with keeping up and should pause and reflect. Since the city is associated with new opportunities, this dream suggests you are hopeful and believe good things are coming your way. Dreaming of working in a city means your job is your number one priority, and it has impacted your relationships with your loved ones. Or you are unsatisfied with your current career and are looking for a change.

Abandoned City

An abandoned city in dreams suggests separation and the end of a relationship. Perhaps you are trying to save your marriage only to realize you are the only one holding on and the other person is no longer interested. This dream is a sign that you should walk away before you start resenting them. Or you will have a huge fight with a loved one that will escalate and end your relationship.

Wandering the City

This dream signifies your indecisive nature. You will struggle with making a choice soon because the two options will appeal to you. You do not want to make the wrong choice and regret it later. This dream is a warning that some people can take advantage of your confusion and influence you to make a choice that benefits them.

Dreaming you are wandering around a strange city suggests you will move to a new country or experience an unfamiliar situation. You will struggle with the change at first, especially if it involves meeting new people. However, in time, you will adapt and embrace your new life.

If you get lost while wandering around a city, it means you're struggling with making a decision related to your career. Perhaps you want to start your own business but are worried about taking the risk. It can also mean you got promoted in your waking life or were assigned a new project, and you feel overwhelmed by your new responsibilities. You find it hard to make any decision because you know it will impact other people. It can also indicate feeling confused in the workplace. Either management or your responsibilities have changed, and you aren't sure what is expected of you anymore.

Countryside

Dreaming about the countryside indicates feeling exhausted and stressed in your waking life. Your relationships and the people in your life can also make you feel constrained. Being in the countryside symbolizes the peace and freedom you crave. You desire to escape from your chaotic life to a quiet and natural environment. The dream further means that you feel free from the rules imposed by society.

Living in the Countryside

Dreaming of living in the countryside indicates that things will work out in your life. You have either found the person you want to spend the rest of your life with or finally found a career that makes you happy. You are finally in control of your life.

Visiting the Countryside

If you dream of visiting the countryside, you require a break or vacation to get away from it all. It can also indicate that you are about to experience positive changes in your life. Whatever is troubling you or causing you stress is about to end.

Forest

Dreaming of a forest may indicate feelings of insecurity.[8]

Dreaming of a forest means you are looking for something that is no longer there. Walking in a forest can indicate feeling insecure and unsettled. It also symbolizes transformation and reflection. Your subconscious is telling you to look inward and reevaluate how you handle life's obstacles and find happiness. It can further mean that you should be aware of your surroundings to protect yourself to prevent problems.

Being in a Forest

Dreaming of being in a forest suggests that you should be cautious. You can have problems at work that require your full attention. It can also indicate that you will experience discord with other family members. This dream can serve as a warning that someone in your life will betray you. Do not share your fear or insecurities with people you don't trust; they can use your weaknesses against you.

Getting Lost in a Forest

This dream is a sign that you will probably experience disappointment and betrayal. It also means that you should be grateful for what you have because circumstances can change at any minute. If you are in a tough position right now, this dream is telling you to learn from the difficulties as they will make you stronger, and things will get better.

Library

Dreaming about a library symbolizes your vast knowledge and wisdom. Your loved ones often seek your advice and trust your opinion. It also indicates that certain information is hidden from you and that some people in your life are not what they seem. Your subconscious is telling you to do more research while being careful and alert to uncover what is hidden. This dream is further telling you to look within to find the answers you seek.

Empty and Abandoned Libraries

Dreaming of an empty library is a sign that you are about to face some trouble in your professional life. Your company may be facing financial problems and have to lay off some people, or your performance may not meet its standards, so you worry they may let you go. Perhaps, one of your co-workers will stab you in the back and cause you to lose your job.

Seeing an abandoned library in your dream implies giving up your professional and academic goals to focus on your family. Your subconscious is telling you to keep chasing your dreams, or you will live with regret.

People in a Library

Dreaming about strangers in a library means you should understand your strengths, weaknesses, and abilities before starting any new project. If you dream about friends or family in a library and this person guides you, you are learning from them in your waking life. They will open your eyes to the knowledge you never even knew existed. If you are alone in a library, it is a sign that you will eventually achieve all your goals.

Long Hallway

Dreaming about a long hallway symbolizes your passion, leadership, enthusiasm, and courage. It also signifies transformation in your life. However, you are not willing to embrace the change. You want everything to stay the same. This dream further symbolizes nostalgia, worries, and insecurity.

Running Down a Long Hallway

This dream suggests poor health or sadness in your waking life. Your subconscious is telling you to slow down and focus on yourself. It indicates that something in your life requires your immediate attention. The dream reflects self-doubt. You do not believe you have what it takes to achieve your goals. It also implies you will experience the end of your business or relationship.

Walking in a Long Hallway

This dream suggests you are about to start a new chapter in your life and should be prepared for it. However, your subconscious is telling you to weigh all your options before making any decision.

Stairs

Stairs dreams signify personal growth and working to achieve your goals. They symbolize the steps you should take to be successful in your waking life. They also reflect the ups and downs you feel in your daily life.

Climbing up the Stairs

Dreaming you are climbing up the stairs symbolizes achieving your dreams. It reflects your ambitious nature. Long stairs mean your goal will not be easy to achieve, and you will face challenges along the way. If you're climbing the stairs with difficulty, you face setbacks in your waking life. Your subconscious may be warning you to pause and take care of yourself.

Going Down the Stairs

This dream signifies stepping down from a high position—like getting demoted at work. It also means that something in your life is stressing you out, and you feel crushed under its weight. Difficulty in climbing down the stairs symbolizes hesitation toward change. If you are easily climbing down the stairs, you are optimistic and confident about the future.

Tunnel

Dreaming about tunnels means you are ready to put the past behind you and focus on the future. They represent the road you take and the challenges you face in life. Tunnels reflect your strong abilities and positive attitude even when you face challenges and hardships. If you have this dream during a hard time in your waking life, your subconscious is sending you a message to stay strong and keep going. Knowing where the tunnel leads in your dream means you feel safe and secure about the path you are taking in your waking life. However, if the route is unclear, you feel uncertain about your choices.

Being in a Tunnel

This dream implies you have overcome challenges in your waking life that prevented you from achieving your goals. Now that you have accomplished them, you are about to go on a new and exciting journey.

Getting Stuck in a Tunnel

Dreaming about getting stuck in a tunnel suggests that a misunderstanding between you and a friend will lead to a huge fight. If the tunnel is dark, you are facing challenges in your life and looking for support. The darkness indicates you're feeling lonely. You're going through tough times and refuse to confide in or open up to anyone.

Every story takes place somewhere, and the stories in your dreams are no different. The location of your dream is a message from your subconscious about the state of your mind. Train yourself to notice where your dreams take place. The more locations you encounter, the more messages you must decipher. Understanding the meaning behind these places will give you an insight into your mind and reveal secrets about yourself that will surprise you. When it comes to interpreting dreams, follow the advice of real estate agents and focus on location, location, location.

Chapter 5: Dream Symbolism of the Four Elements

Symbols have been used throughout history to represent abstract concepts and feelings, and dreams are no exception. Dream symbolism in the four elements, fire, earth, water, and air, is an ancient Grecian technique of connecting with the natural world. In a dream, each element represents something unique. Whether you dream of a raging fire, a lush tropical beach, or a powerful gust of wind, the elements offer a unique way of understanding your innermost thoughts and feelings. This chapter will explore why understanding these elements' symbolism can help decipher the meaning of your dreams and gain a deeper insight into your subconscious.

The Four Elements

The origin of the four elements in dreams can be traced back to ancient Greece. This belief system, called the Four Elements Theory, was founded circa 450 BC and later taken up by Aristotle. It suggested that all matter on Earth was composed of four fundamental elements: Fire, water, earth, and air. According to ancient Greece, dreams were a manifestation of the four elements of the universe.

1. Fire was believed to be the element of creativity and passion
2. Water was associated with emotions and the unconscious
3. Earth was linked to physical reality

4. Air was connected to the spiritual realm

For the ancient Greeks, the four elements were essential to understand the human experience, and the dreaming process was an extension of this. This theory was integral to the development of Western philosophy and has been adopted by many cultures around the world. Today, the four elements are still used as an intrinsic aspect of dream interpretation.

- Fire is often seen in dreams as a symbol of passion, energy, strength, and creativity. It represents drive, ambition, and motivation. Fire can be a sign of a burning desire or a warning to be careful about something that could be dangerous.
- Earth is associated with stability, groundedness, and practicality. A reminder to stay in tune with the present moment and stay focused on what is important, earth represents your connection to the physical world and others.
- Water is an element of emotion, intuition, and creativity. It reflects your innermost feelings, as well as your subconscious desires. Water is also a sign of being open to change or learning from past experiences.
- Air is associated with communication, clarity, and freedom. A sign of needing to express yourself openly or being open to new ideas and perspectives, air represents a need for clarity in a difficult situation.

Let us take a deeper look into each of the four elements so you can assess the overall energy of your dream and get an in-depth insight into the dream's potential message and purpose.

Fire

Fire is a powerful symbol with a wide range of interpretations. From passion and transformation to destruction and anger, the symbolism of fire depends on the context of the dream, your feelings, and your current state of mind. A dream featuring a raging fire might symbolize:

- Intense emotions, such as anger, rage, or passion.
- A powerful transformation, such as a new beginning or a rebirth.
- Warmth, comfort, and security.

Fire can also be a symbol of destruction. If the dreamer is feeling overwhelmed or facing a difficult situation, fire may be warning them of danger ahead or represent the destruction that could happen if the dreamer is not careful. The color of the fire can be significant, too:

- Bright yellow or orange fire may represent energy, warmth, and passion.
- Red fire may symbolize anger or rage.
- Blue fire may represent a spiritual transformation or calming influence.

House Fire

Dreams about house fires are often interpreted as a sign of fear or anxiety. Fire symbolism is linked to insecurity, vulnerability, and anger, as well as indicating a lack of control and a deep-seated desire to take more charge of your life. The dream suggests:

- Lack of control.
- A situation that you feel powerless to change.
- A sign of destructive impulses or habits that you need to get rid of.
- Potential danger.
- That you are feeling overwhelmed.

Because fire is associated with transformation, destruction, and renewal, a house fire can symbolize:

- A desire to make a fresh start or a period of transition.
- Aspects of your life that need to be addressed or changed.
- Passion and intensity, so it could be representative of strong emotions.

Being Close to a Fire/Fire in the Distance

If you dream of being near a burning fire, it means you feel overwhelmed by intense emotions and need to find a way to express yourself.

- If you light the fire yourself in your dream, you strongly desire to create something new or start a new project. It also indicates that you need to take control of your life and be more assertive.
- On the other hand, if the fire in your dream is already lit, you feel energized and ready to take on new challenges.

Dreaming about a burning fire in the distance signifies an impending crisis or a warning of potential danger.

- If you are feeling conflicted or are struggling with something, the fire represents the intensity of the situation, and the distance represents how far away a solution feels.

A fire in the distance also symbolizes your passion and enthusiasm for something in your life, but you have yet to put in the work to achieve it. Nonetheless, your enthusiasm and passion burn brightly, and you are making progress toward achieving something.

You are on Fire

Dreaming about being on fire yourself is a sign of transformation and rebirth. This type of dream often indicates that you're going through a period of personal growth and development. It also signifies a desire to make changes in your life, such as changing careers or starting a new relationship, but you're afraid of failure or of being judged by others. Ultimately, the symbolism of this dream could be interpreted in different ways, depending on the context and the details of the dream. For example:

- If you dream of being engulfed in flames and feeling a sense of freedom, it means that you're ready to take risks and make bold changes in your life.
- Alternatively, if you feel overwhelmed by the flames, it is a sign that you're overwhelmed by life's challenges or feel stuck in an unsatisfying situation.

Someone Else is on Fire

Dreams about someone else being on fire could be a source of confusion and fear. It can be difficult to wrap your head around the symbolism of such a dream, especially if it involves someone you love. Whatever the case, remember that these dreams are symbolic and should not be taken at face value. Take the time to reflect on what the dreams mean and how they apply to you. In dream symbolism, someone else being on fire can indicate a need for change or transformation in your life:

- It is a sign of anger or resentment toward them and means that you must confront them and have an honest conversation.
- It is a sign of wishful thinking or a desire to see that person suffer in some way.

- It is a sign that you need to let go of something holding you back, whether it's a toxic relationship or a destructive habit

Essentially, dreams like this symbolize the end of a particular phase in your life or the start of something new and exciting. However, you must address whatever is holding you back before moving forward.

Earth

Generally, when you dream of earth, it symbolizes stability and security. Specifically, this indicates the need to stay grounded and connected to one's roots. It can remind one to stay true to oneself and one's values. Earth also represents:

- Fertility and growth, suggesting that the dreamer is in a good place in their life and can manifest their dreams and desires.
- A warning to focus on the present, as the dreamer's actions now will determine the future.
- A sign of abundance and prosperity, as the earth is abundant and always provides what is necessary.

The symbolism of earth in dreams is related to one's mother and family. It serves as a reminder that one must take care of family or cherish the time they have with them. As the earth is the ultimate nurturer, it represents the need for nurturing and compassion.

A Natural Disaster

Dreaming about natural disasters such as earthquakes, floods, hurricanes, and tornadoes can be interpreted in various ways, depending on the details of the dream. For example:

- If you dream of an earthquake, it represents an upheaval in your life. This could be something big, such as a move or a new job, or something smaller, such as the end of a relationship.
- Dreaming of a flood represents an emotional release. It symbolizes an overwhelming sense of emotions that you have been holding back.
- Alternatively, if you dream of seeing a flood, it is a sign of letting go of something holding you back, such as a toxic relationship or an unhealthy habit.

- Dreaming of a hurricane, tornado, or other powerful storm represents a period of intense growth or transformation. The storm's intensity indicates the level of transformation that you are going through. If the storm was destructive, it means the end of an old chapter, while if it was calming, it means a new beginning is about to unfold.

Depending on how you felt during the dream, you can take these natural disaster scenarios as positive or negative. If you feel scared and helpless, it represents a lack of control over your life. On the other hand, if you feel energized and ready to face the danger, it represents a willingness to embrace new opportunities.

Being Buried

When you dream of being buried in the earth, it could mean a variety of different things depending on the context of the dream:

- A desire to escape from a difficult situation.
- Being overwhelmed.
- A desire to be protected from the outside world.
- The feeling of being stuck in life.
- A desire to be closer to nature.
- A feeling of being weighed down by the responsibilities of life.

When it comes to dream symbolism like this, consider the context of the dream and how you felt when you woke up. If you felt relief or a sense of liberation, the dream represents a desire to escape a difficult situation. If the dream left you feeling helpless or overwhelmed, it means you are overwhelmed. On the other hand, if the dream left you feeling safe and secure, it represents a desire to be protected from the outside world.

Seeing the Planets in the Sky

Dreams can be a fascinating and mysterious phenomenon. When you dream about seeing the planets in the sky, it can be a reflection of your innermost thoughts and emotions. These types of dreams symbolize:

- Ambition, exploration, and a desire to reach the stars.
- The need to expand your horizons and explore the world.
- A desire to better understand yourself and the world around you.

- Being overwhelmed by the enormity of life and the responsibilities that come with it. Your subconscious is telling you to take a step back and reassess the direction in which you are heading.

Looking Down on Earth from Space

Dreaming of looking down on Earth from space is a powerful symbol of perspective and spiritual and physical distance. It represents understanding, clarity, and distance from your current situation. Your subconscious is telling you to look at a situation from a different angle, to take a step back, and gain some emotional distance. Seeing Earth from space represents:

- The need for spiritual growth and development.
- A reminder to take some time out of your busy life and spend it with yourself or nature.
- A sign to take a break from technology and reconnect with yourself and the natural world, allowing yourself to gain a new perspective.
- The need for physical distance or change.

Water

When you dream of water, it indicates an emotional state—feelings such as calmness, tranquility, balance, fear, anxiety, and turbulence. Water talks to the depths of your subconscious mind, which can be dark and mysterious, symbolizing feelings you cannot express in your waking life. Water also represents:

- Spiritual cleansing and renewal.
- A sign of awakening and spiritual growth.
- New beginnings and opportunities.
- A journey of transformation.

Finally, dreaming of water in any state implies a connection to the divine: A sign of being in tune with your higher self, which means you are ready to make positive changes.

The Ocean

Dreaming of the ocean may indicate emotional expressiveness.[9]

If you are swimming, sailing, or floating in the ocean, viewing it from afar or close up, this typically indicates that something is being released or washed away or that you're in the process of expressing yourself emotionally. It is also a sign of spiritual cleansing or a connection with the unknown. Because the ocean symbolizes the vastness of the unconscious and the inner depths of the soul, dreaming about it reminds you to trust your intuition and instincts and explore your depths. In some cases, dreaming about the ocean indicates a fear of the unknown or being overwhelmed by emotions or stress. Dreaming about the ocean represents:

- Growth and transformation.
- A new stage in life.
- A period of healing and renewal.
- A source of life and abundance in the near future.

Lakes and Rivers

Dreaming about lakes and rivers can be interpreted as a spiritual journey toward understanding yourself and finding your inner peace. More deeply, dreaming about lakes and rivers can represent transformation, renewal, and fertility. This is because their flowing nature symbolizes the subconscious, the unknown, and the depths of our inner selves. Dreaming about lakes and rivers suggests:

- That you are searching for a deeper understanding of yourself.
- That you are looking to tap into your inner wisdom.
- A sign of creativity and inspiration.
- An association with emotional healing and the need to let go of the past.

Because the river and lake water represent the tears you may need to shed to move on from a difficult situation, dreaming about them means you need emotional release. They are a place of emotional safety and security for you to rest and heal.

Rain

Rain in dreams symbolizes cleansing and renewal, suggesting a time for change and new beginnings. If you feel like your life has been stagnant or dull, the rain in your dream shows that you need to shake things up and make a change. Or at least take a break and start fresh. In some cases, dreaming about rain indicates:

- Sadness and grief.
- An expression of your emotions and a sign that you need to take some time to process and heal.
- You need to take a step back and find a new perspective.
- You need to pay closer attention to your intuition and look for signs from the universe.
- You need to pay more attention to your feelings and trust your inner voice.

If you have been struggling with a project or problem, rain in your dream indicates success. It means your financial situation is about to improve, or your hard work will soon pay off.

Drowning

Dreams of drowning can be quite unsettling. However, it is a powerful reminder to pay attention to your feelings and take control of the situation. These feelings are related to the current state of your life or a particular problem or issue. When you dream that you're drowning, it means that you're feeling like you cannot keep your head above water. You may feel like you're stuck and do not know how to get out. This symbolism is closely related to feelings of being overwhelmed by a particular problem or the general chaos of life.

In some cases, it is a sign that you're trying to avoid facing a difficult situation or a problem you've been avoiding. The dream is telling you that you need to take control and deal with the issue to move forward.

Air

Air symbolizes freedom in dreams. As a symbol of liberation, creativity, and joy, if you dream of flying or soaring through the air, it is a sign that you are feeling emotional or spiritual freedom. Alternatively, dreams about air represent:

- Being overwhelmed.
- The need to take a mental or spiritual break.
- Communication, ideas, and thoughts.
- A connection with a higher power or your intuition.
- A sign that you need to open your mind to new ideas and possibilities.
- Spiritual understanding.

Suffocating

Dreams can be very mysterious, and interpreting them can be even more puzzling. However, dreaming of being suffocated has a very clear message: Your subconscious is trying to tell you that you are feeling overwhelmed by something in your waking life. Suffocating in a dream symbolizes feeling stifled by a situation or person or that you cannot make progress and express yourself in some area of your life. You ma feel trapped, whether it is in your job, a relationship, or a situation that you are unable to control. Dreams of this nature also mean:

- You feel your opinion or feelings are not being considered or respected.

These feelings of being overwhelmed can be quite daunting and could be the cause of your subconscious trying to express these feelings in your dream.

Feeling a Breeze

Dreaming about feeling a nice breeze is a sign of contentment and a symbol of a pleasant change coming your way. It also signifies a feeling of freedom, joy, and hope, as the wind is associated with liberation. A nice breeze can represent:

- A new beginning, a new journey, or a fresh start.
- The presence of a spiritual guide or an angel watching over you and helping you on your journey.
- That you are about to experience a peaceful period in your life.

On a deeper level, dreaming about feeling a nice breeze signifies that something positive is coming your way. As a symbol of progress, success, and happiness, dreams like this mean you are moving in the right direction and are manifesting your dreams into reality.

Something Flying in Your Face

Dreaming about something flying in your face can be a scary experience, especially if it is one of those that jump scare you awake. But when they happen, they are a symbol of your fear of failure or fear of a certain situation in your life. Other meanings include:

- Something is coming your way that you are not prepared for.
- A situation that you're trying to avoid.
- You need to be more open and vulnerable in your life.
- You need to take a risk and be willing to face whatever comes your way.

Coming Up against a Storm, Flying Dirt, or Heavy Wind

Dreams about coming up against a storm, dirt, or heavy wind symbolize a chaotic situation in your waking life. Representing a situation in which you feel overwhelmed and out of control, dreams like this reflect stress and turmoil.

- A storm or wind is connected to the idea of change, a period of upheaval and rapid transformation.
- Dirt flying in your face is connected to new beginnings. A sign that you are ready to start fresh and make a new beginning.

Learning about dream symbolism of the four elements is an incredibly insightful and meaningful exercise. Each element—fire, earth, water, and air—holds a unique set of symbols and meanings. By understanding the symbolism of these four elements, you will get a deeper understanding of the hidden messages and meanings in your dreams. By uncovering your subconscious desires and fears and the deeper aspects of your life, you'll be on your way to a journey of self-discovery.

Chapter 6: Looking at Colors and Numbers

Dreams can be filled with strange symbols and images that initially seem nonsensical. Colors and numbers often appear and have special meanings. Colors associated with hidden emotions provide insights into your subconscious mind. Numbers, on the other hand, represent spiritual guidance and enlightenment. This chapter will explore the symbolism of colors and numbers in dream interpretation and how to use this analysis to unlock deeper meaning and gain insight into yourself.

Colors

When dreaming about colors, there is no single meaning or interpretation. Every person has a very personal experience and relationship with colors, so the explanation varies from person to person. However, in general, colors express emotions. They provide a framework for emotional insight and indicate a positive or negative outlook or feeling:

- Green symbolizes balance, harmony, growth, and fertility
- Blue signifies peace and tranquility
- Yellow symbolizes optimism and joy
- Red signifies anger, passion, or danger
- Black means sadness, grief, fear, and negativity

- White indicates a sense of purity, innocence, sterility, or emptiness
- Orange sky refers to optimism and enthusiasm Colors that represent specific memories and events from your past: Vivid yellow symbolizes nostalgia for a certain time in your life Color in dreams can be used to help you to understand your subconscious mind:Bright pink symbolizes a need for more love and nurturing in your life
- Deep green suggests a need for more inner balance and harmony

Ultimately, the meaning of colors in dreams is highly subjective and dependent on the individual. As you delve into the specifics of the following dream scenarios, consider the context of the dream, as well as how you feel during and after. Then, reflect on the recent events that have occurred in your life, as they may have influenced your dream in some way.

Black

Black is mysterious and powerful. It represents the unknown, shadows, and your subconscious. Often associated with strength and fortitude, black symbolizes protection, transformation, and strength.

- A dream in which everything appears in shades of black represents darkness and the unknown, suggesting a sense of fear.
- All black refers to a period of darkness before growth and light.
- If you are in a dark room, it represents disorientation and confusion.
- If the dream includes a black cat, it symbolizes bad luck or deception.
- Dreams of a black horse mean power and freedom.
- A black sky means death, either literal or metaphorical one, such as the death of an old habit or behavior.

Blue

Blue is the color of peace, tranquility, and deep understanding. Dreams with this color symbolize truth, faith, and communication and indicate that you feel emotionally calm and secure. Following that, blue in a dream often represents a positive feeling or desire to find inner peace.

- A bright blue sky symbolizes a sense of freedom and openness.
- A soothing blue ocean represents calming emotions and a desire to stay grounded.
- Blue clothes, either yours or someone else's, symbolize security and protection.

Brown

Brown is a color of stability and practicality. It signifies organization, structure, and a connection to the natural world. Dreaming of brown can indicate a desire for something reliable. Essentially, you're looking for stability.

- A tree trunk symbolizes a need for grounding and stability.
- If you dream of a barren landscape, you are uninspired and lack motivation.
- Brown dirt on your hands refers to feeling lost. It means that you're feeling disoriented and need help finding your way.
- A brown suitcase symbolizes a journey.
- A brown car means success.
- A brown river represents the flow of life.
- A brown bird represents good luck or fortune.

Burgundy

Burgundy is a deep, rich color and symbolizes passion, ambition, and intensity. It represents courage, strength, and determination. Dreams featuring burgundy are often a sign that you are feeling empowered and motivated to take on a new challenge. In dreams, this appears as self-empowerment and strength:

- A burgundy dress symbolizes that you are taking control of your life or are about to embark on a new journey.
- If a car is burgundy, it means that you are driving your destiny and controlling where you are going.
- Walls of burgundy represent a barrier or protection from outside forces.
- A person in burgundy symbolizes that you are meeting a powerful and inspiring figure in your life.

Cream

Associated with innocence and purity, cream symbolizes a new beginning or fresh start. When cream is seen in a dream, it indicates a desire to be free from something or to start over. From a psychological perspective, cream is also associated with comfort and security, or the need for healing:

- A cream-colored blanket is a sign that you need to take time for yourself and relax.
- If you dream of a cream-colored wall, it's a sign that you feel trapped and need to find a way to break free.
- A cream-colored sky symbolizes peace and tranquility.

Gold

Gold is associated with wealth, power, and success. Indicating a desire for material possessions or a need for recognition or respect, gold means you have ambition, a drive for success, or a wish to be seen as important or valuable.

- A golden pot of coins means that you will soon become wealthy.
- A gold ring symbolizes commitment and long-term success.
- Other gold things in a dream can include golden statues, jewelry, and even clothing.

Regardless of its form, gold usually signifies something positive in your life.

Green

Green, the symbol of growth, fertility, and nature, indicates a hope for the future or a desire for abundance. When green appears in a dream, it is a sign that you are on the right path and need to trust your instincts and follow your dreams. Green has a calming effect, so it is no surprise that it appears in your dreams. From lush green meadows to emerald-colored lakes, green is a common sight in the dream world:

- A green tree symbolizes the growth of a relationship.
- A green field foretells an abundance of wealth and success.
- A ray of green light signifies hope.
- Green clothing is a sign of fertility or abundance.
- Green eyes symbolize intuition and knowledge.

Ivory

Ivory, the color of purity and innocence, symbolizes peace, tranquility, and balance. When ivory appears in a dream, it is a sign that you are in a place of security and comfort.

- If you see someone wearing an ivory gown, it symbolizes a need for spiritual purity.
- An ivory statue is a sign that you're ready to let go of something in the past and move on to something new.
- An ivory wall indicates that you're ready to build a new foundation in your life and create something fresh and exciting.

Lilac

The color lilac may indicate a dreamer's naivety.[10]

Lilac is associated with joy and youthfulness. In a dream, this color represents the dreamer's innocence and naivety about a situation or person. It also signifies a need to break away from a situation and explore new opportunities. Dreams featuring things that are lilac can be quite telling as this color often has strong connotations:

- A lilac-colored sky indicates that you feel peaceful and content with the current state of your life.
- Lilac-colored flowers are a sign that you need more joy and beauty and are looking for ways to bring more of these into your life.

- A lilac-colored house means you seek a more harmonious and balanced home life.

Maroon

Maroon is often seen as a sign of power and authority. In a dream, this color represents the need to take control. It can signify a desire to be respected and admired. Dreams featuring things that are maroon can be interpreted as a sign of deep transformation, strength, and wisdom:

- A maroon sky indicates a dark period of your life.
- A maroon wall symbolizes a barrier preventing you from achieving your goals.
- Maroon clothing signifies a deep desire to be accepted or respected. It could also be a sign of feeling vulnerable.
- Maroon furniture is a sign of stagnation and lack of growth.

Maroon is also seen in dreams in the form of animals:

- A maroon snake indicates that you are facing a challenge you must overcome.
- A maroon bird represents transformation and freedom.

Mauve

Mauve is often associated with romance and tranquility. This color represents the need to find inner peace and relaxation in a dream. It also signifies a desire for meaningful connections. The color with a dreamy, mysterious vibe appears in dreams in many different forms. From a delicate mauve sunset to a deep mauve ocean, it signifies a range of emotions and feelings:

- A mauve sky represents peace and tranquility.
- On the other hand, a deep mauve ocean represents unease and even fear.

Orange

Orange is a sign of creativity and enthusiasm. In a dream, this color represents a desire for self-expression and the cultivation of ideas. It also signifies a desire to be more open and adventurous. Generally speaking, dreaming of orange things can be interpreted as a new opportunity or an exciting change on the horizon:

- A vivid orange sunset is a sign that you are about to embark on a new adventure.

- Orange flames represent a warning to take caution in some aspects of your life.

Peach

Peach is associated with contentment and happiness. In a dream, this color represents the need for balance and harmony. It also symbolizes a desire for stability and security. This warm, inviting hue can be interpreted in many ways, depending on the context of the dream and the person:

- For some, a peach-colored sky implies a sense of peace, calmness, and contentment.
- For others, if something usually white or gray is colored peach in a dream, it suggests something negative, like a warning against danger or a sign of illness.

Peach is also symbolic of fertility and abundance. For example, a person might dream of eating a peach and feeling full and satisfied.

Pink

Pink is seen as a sign of love and compassion. In a dream, this color represents the need to open up and show true feelings. It also refers to a desire for emotional closeness and intimacy.

- A pink teddy bear could be interpreted as a sign of comfort and security.
- Similarly, dreaming of a pink flower represents growth and rebirth.

  On the other hand, pink is an indicator of something negative:
- A pink sky symbolizes a warning to the dreamer to be more cautious in the near future.
- A pink elephant represents anxiety or fear.

Red

Red is the color of passion, power, love, and anger. In dreams, it is a sign of intense emotions like fear or anger or the presence of a powerful force. A dream featuring lots of red can be a warning to take heed and pay attention to what is going on in your life.

- A red sky is a sign of danger and a warning to be careful.
- Red fruits symbolize the growth of new life.
- Blood represents death or the shedding of old ideas.

- A red rose symbolizes love and passion.
- A red stop sign symbolizes danger to come.

Silver

As the color of luxury, silver is associated with spiritual protection and the presence of divine guidance. It can be a sign that you are being held and supported even in times of difficulty.

- A silver moon refers to intuition and spiritual connection.
- A silver car is a sign of success.
- A silver ring symbolizes commitment.

White

White is the color of purity and innocence. In dreams, it represents new beginnings and a fresh start. It can be a sign of hope and optimism and that you have the power to make positive changes in your life.

- White doves are a sign of peace and protection.
- White clouds indicate a higher spiritual plane.
- White animals, such as horses or lions, represent strength and courage.
- White objects such as houses, castles, or furniture reflect the dreamer's home life, positively or negatively.

Yellow

The color yellow signifies joy, optimism, happiness, and good fortune. A sign of new beginnings and a bright future means you are ready to take on new opportunities and challenges.

- A yellow sky is a sign of hope.
- A yellow river symbolizes intense emotions.
- A yellow dress indicates a desire for change.
- Yellow shoes are a sign of adventure.
- A yellow car is a sign of luxury and good fortune to come.

Numbers

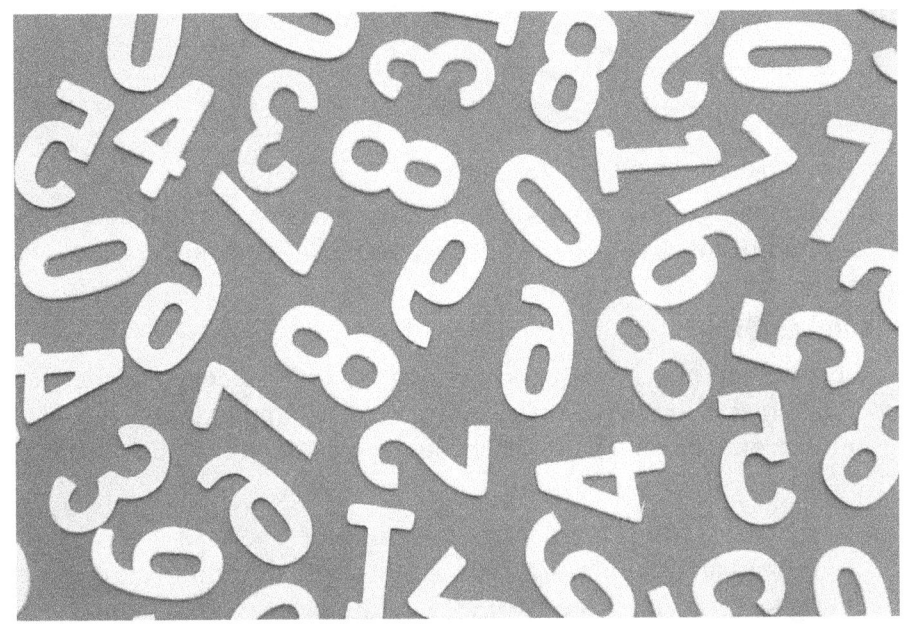

Numbers in a dream can represent many things.[11]

Dreams are a fascinating phenomenon, and they, more often than not, leave us wondering what they mean. Have you ever had a dream where numbers appeared? If so, you are not alone. Many people report dreaming about numbers. But what do these numbers mean? Numbers can represent:

- The passage of time, a countdown, a deadline, or a warning of sorts
- Your subconscious
- Guidance
- An area of your life that needs improvement Specific digits mean something, too: The number three symbolizes creativity, growth, and expansion
- The number four represents stability and structure
- The number seven reflects spiritual understanding

Sometimes, numbers in dreams are literal. They could represent something significant in your life or act as a reminder of things you need to do:

- A phone number
- An address
- A bank account

Pay attention to the context and emotions of your dream and the specific number that appears. This way, you will better understand what your inner self is trying to tell you.

Number One

The number one symbolizes uniqueness, independence, leadership, self-confidence, and strength of character. For example, if you dream of the number one, it could signify that you need to take on a leadership role or take decisive action.

- Dreaming of a clock with the number one is a sign of great potential and success, often hinting that the time has come to take a risk and achieve something extraordinary.
- A sequence of 111 represents a trifecta of positive energy, a triplet of new beginnings, or the idea of a powerful trinity.

Number Two

A symbol of partnership and balance, dreams with the number two suggest the need for collaboration and harmony. It means you need to look for a partner or collaborator to help you reach your goals.

- The number two, in any form, is associated with a financial situation, such as having two sources of income or a bank balance with two digits.

Number Three

A sign of creativity, imagination, growth, and spiritual development, dreaming about the number three is a sign that you need to embrace your creativity and tap into your spiritual side.

- A telephone number that contains the number three signifies you are on the verge of achieving a goal.
- A cloud formation with the number three signifies creativity and abundance.

- A random object with the number three signifies you are about to embark on a new journey.

Number Four

The number four typically symbolizes stability and structure. Representing the four pillars of life—physical, mental, emotional, and spiritual—a dream with the number four is telling you to focus on stability and work on your life's foundations. When the number four appears in your dream, it is related to something practical and significant:

- Seeing a telephone number with the number four indicates that someone needs to contact you urgently or has a secret they want to tell you.
- Dreaming of a calendar with the number four indicates a looming deadline or an event that should not be missed.

Number Five

The number five represents change. As a symbol of transition or transformation, a dream with the number five in it tells you to embrace change and be open to new experiences.

- Five clocks signify impending stress or a reminder to stay in control of your time.
- A five-dollar bill is a sign that you're seeking financial stability or are feeling financially secure.
- A pentagram (a five-pointed star) indicates the need to reconcile innermost feelings and emotions.
- Five doors suggest the need to explore different paths in life.
- Five candles represent the need to be more aware of the spiritual realm.
- Five sticks of dynamite indicate a need for a dramatic change or transformation in life.

Number Six

Often associated with harmony and balance, the number six represents stability, peace, and balance. A dream with the number six in it is telling you to focus on achieving harmony and balance in your life.

- Six objects, such as six chairs or books, signify a need for balance or stability.

- Six children suggest a desire to be surrounded by love and support.
- A six-leafed clover suggests that you have the luck of the Irish on your side.
- A six-sided die symbolizes a desire to take a gamble and risk something for a potential reward.

Number Seven

Lucky number seven. Dreams with this number can be interpreted as a sign of good luck and fortune coming your way.

- Seven birds are a sign of good luck and success coming your way.
- Seven stars in the sky represent spiritual enlightenment.
- Seven coins signify the need to be more mindful of your finances.

Number Eight

The number eight is also seen as a powerful and auspicious number in many cultures, and it can symbolize abundance and prosperity. Dreams of the number eight signify that you will have many resources at your disposal and are on the right path.

- Eight people could mean that you are surrounded by supportive, caring people in your life.
- Eight objects mean you're trying to achieve something or a reminder to stay focused on your goal.

Number Nine

Very telling, the number nine is a sign that you're on the brink of achieving something important. It could mean you're on the cusp of a breakthrough and should keep pushing forward.

- The number nine as a date means you are nearing the end of something that has been occupying your life for some time.
- The number nine on your clock is a powerful reminder that it is time to look forward and start afresh.

Learning about colors and numbers is an interesting and exciting experience. There is much to explore, from the symbolic meanings of colors to how numbers can be interpreted. For instance, the symbolic meaning of colors gives you tremendous insight into your subconscious. On the other hand, numbers can be used to explore a variety of energies, from the physical world to spiritual and metaphysical realms. Thus, learning about colors and numbers can be a great way to gain a better understanding of your inner workings.

Chapter 7: Dreams with Animals and Plants

Have you ever had a dream which involved animals or plants? Animals, primarily, and plants, secondarily, are common symbols that appear in dreams, and they can have a variety of meanings. This chapter will cover the extensive symbolic meaning of dreaming about animals and plants. It will explore why these symbols may appear in your dreamscapes, what kind of messages or insights they could offer you, and how to interpret them.

Animals in Dreams

Animals often appear in dreams as symbols giving us greater insight into the unconscious and spiritual realms. Different animals represent distinct aspects of yourself, such as power, intuition, aggression, innocence, flightiness, or wisdom. They also represent a specific trait or feeling you strive to learn or embody. Paying attention to the animals in your dreams can be valuable for personal growth and self-discovery.

The animal in your dream can be a clue to its meaning. Different species have different symbolic connotations; understanding them is key to interpreting your dream.

Lion

The lion is a powerful and majestic symbol of strength, courage, and leadership. In dreams, it depicts the power and self-confidence required in your daily life. Alternatively, it symbolizes feeling or being trapped in an uncomfortable situation. It represents a need to act or make decisions to progress.

The lion also symbolizes primal fear and instinct. It often represents a deep inner fear or anxiety you may struggle to overcome. In some cases, this can be a fear of the unknown or a fear of change.

The lion is further associated with royalty and nobility, a symbol of power, strength, and authority in many cultures. In dream interpretation, it can indicate the need to be more assertive or take on a leadership role in your life. It also represents a desire for recognition or admiration from others.

Cat

Cats are symbols of mystery, magic, playfulness, and independence. They represent your inner wildness and capacity for autonomy, resourcefulness, and survival. They additionally symbolize your ability to hide and protect yourself from the outside world.

In a dream, cats can be seen as a sign of protection and symbolize your spiritual connection to the world. They represent an independent spirit or the ability to care for yourself. They could also represent mystery, intuition, and the unknown.

Dreams about cats are often echoes of your internal emotions, feelings, and desires. It is a message to connect with your intuition and inner wisdom. Moreover, dreams of cats can be interpreted as signs of your hidden potential and intuition.

Dog

Dreams about dogs often symbolize loyalty, companionship, and protection. Depending on the type of dog in the dream, it can be a sign of faithfulness or even possessiveness. It could represent innocence and playfulness if you dream of a small dog like a poodle or terrier. If you are dreaming of larger dogs, such as a German shepherd, it can symbolize strength and courage. If the dog is barking in your dream, it could indicate your need to defend yourself against someone or something. It could also represent a warning about potential danger coming your way.

Horse

Dreams about horses symbolize power and energy. Horses have long been associated with strong emotions like passion and freedom. If the horse is wild, it can represent wild energy that needs to be tamed. If the horse is calm and content in your dream, this reflects your emotional state and how you deal with strong emotions.

Dreams about horses can also be interpreted as a desire for freedom or movement. The horse may represent a need for change and growth in your life. Alternatively, the dream could tell you that it is time to step out of your comfort zone and take risks to achieve success. Horses can also represent your ambition, desire for power, or need to control your destiny. If the horse appears galloping in your dream, you are feeling powerful and capable of achieving success.

Some believe that the dreams of horses can also be interpreted as a sign of good luck and fortune. If the horse appears strong and healthy, this may indicate a prosperous future. Alternatively, if the horse is weak or dying in your dream, this could mean that difficult times are ahead.

Dreaming of a white horse could be interpreted as a spiritual sign, representing your inner spirit or higher self. Such dreams suggest your need to embrace a spiritual journey to reach enlightenment. If the horse is black, this could indicate ambition and power. Overall, the meaning of a dream with horses depends on many variables, such as color, behavior, and the overall context of your dream.

Elephant

Elephants are seen as a sign of protection.[12]

In dream interpretation, elephants represent strength, power, wisdom, and luck. They can be seen as a sign of protection. Dreaming of an elephant indicates good luck and fortune coming your way soon. It also suggests that you should be prepared for hard work and difficulties coming up in your life. Elephants represent strength and courage, which could signify that you are ready to take on any challenge.

In some cultures, elephants represent fertility and abundance. Dreaming of an elephant could mean you are ready to start a new chapter and open yourself up to all the possibilities it will bring. If the elephant is big, it could symbolize that you have much to offer and a great capacity for growth.

Bear

Bears represent strength and potential for courage. They often symbolize protection, so dreaming of a bear could be interpreted as a sign of protection from something in your life. Bears can also signify your need to take on more responsibility or assert yourself within your relationships or family.

Raccoon

In dream interpretation, raccoons symbolize craftiness and cleverness. They indicate that you need to use your problem-solving and critical thinking skills to find a creative solution to an issue you may face. If a raccoon appears in your dream, it can represent your lack of security and uncertainty. It could also mean hiding something from others or protecting yourself from potential danger. On a more positive note, a raccoon in your dream signifies the importance of adapting to your environment and being flexible.

More generally, raccoons symbolize the need to look at a situation from multiple perspectives and use intuition to reach the right solution.

Each animal has its singular symbolism and meaning, so paying attention to the details in your dream is essential. Pay close attention to any animal in your dream, as it could have a special message just for you. To put the qualities of animals succinctly:

- **Lion:** Power, courage, and leadership
- **Tiger:** Strength and aggression
- **Dog:** Loyalty and protection
- **Elephant:** Wisdom, patience, and kindness
- **Mice:** Timidity and meekness
- **Butterfly:** Transformation and rebirth

- **Frogs:** Fearlessness in new things
- **Birds:** Reaching for greater heights
- **Hawk:** Visionary qualities and the ability to rise above
- **Owl:** Intuition, insight, and clairvoyance
- **Horse:** Strength, freedom, and the power to take control
- **Wolf:** Resourcefulness and instinctual power
- **Unicorn:** Magic, hope, and ability to transcend
- **Fish:** Intuition, creativity, and emotions
- **Reptiles (snakes or dragons):** Unknown fears and hidden truths

Dreams about Bugs

Bugs in dreams often represent feeling out of control, overwhelmed, or vulnerable. They symbolize a fear of the unknown or feeling insignificant in the grand scheme. Bugs often appear in dreams when you feel your life is spiraling out of control and you are struggling to keep up with all the changes around you.

Dreams about bugs signify the presence of a problem or issue that is causing you stress. It may also mean something in your life needs to be addressed or dealt with.

Ants

Dreams about ants signify hard work, determination, and perseverance in achieving your goals. Ants are often seen scurrying around in an organized manner, which can symbolize a need to get organized to achieve your goals. Ants can also represent industriousness, ambition, and productivity.

Spiders

Dreams about spiders often signify a need to look more closely at something in your life and ensure that you see it from all angles. Spiders can also represent your intuition and ability to sense danger, or they may be a warning of something being hidden from you.

If you dream of a spider crawling on your body, it may indicate someone is trying to take advantage of you. Alternatively, it could mean a part of your life you neglect, such as an unhealthy relationship or toxic habit. This dream may encourage you to look at this area and make changes.

Dreams of being trapped in a spider's web signify that you feel stuck in a particular situation or relationship. You may think that you cannot get out of the web, and no matter how hard you struggle, you cannot escape. This dream asks you to look within yourself and understand why you feel trapped before trying to change your life.

Bees

Dreams about bees indicate hard work, ambition, and productivity. They can signify your enthusiasm for projects or activities that you are working on. Bees represent the pollinating power of hard work and the importance of working together to accomplish tasks and projects. When you see a bee or swarm of bees in your dream, it is a sign that you are working hard to achieve something. It reminds you to focus on the task before you and strive to reach your goals.

Dreams with bees also symbolize that someone's negative energy is being directed at you and their attempts to disrupt your success. If you dream of a swarm of bees coming at you, it could indicate that someone is trying to interfere in your life or stop you from achieving your goals.

Fleas

Dreams about fleas often signify feeling overwhelmed and helpless in a certain situation. Fleas can also represent being irritated by someone or something but not having the power to do anything about it.

Cockroaches

Dreams about cockroaches often signify feeling powerless and helpless in the face of a problem. They can also symbolize feeling dirty and disgusting or having a physical or emotional issue that needs to be addressed.

Flies

Dreams about flies often represent feelings of being swamped and overwhelmed. They represent feeling powerless or unable to stop something from happening. Flies can be an annoyance in the dream, often indicating a feeling of being pestered or harassed by someone. In some cases, flies could represent a feeling of being a victim to someone or something. Alternatively, if the flies are orderly and not bothering you, it could be a sign of good luck.

Wasps

Dreams about wasps often represent difficult and uninviting situations. It could be a sign that you are feeling overwhelmed by a problem in your life or facing resistance from someone. Wasps can sometimes be a warning of danger or that something terrible is about to happen. They signify aggression, betrayal, or tension in your relationships.

Wasps can also be seen as a sign of pride or ego. You may find yourself feeling overly confident about your abilities or particularly ambitious. This is a message that you must take a step back and assess the situation before making significant decisions.

The context of the dream is also consequential; for example, a lion might have different meanings depending on whether it is in a zoo or attacking you. In the former case, it could mean your strength is being caged in or restricted somehow. It might signify a need to confront your inner demons in the latter. Similarly, the location of the dream is also important. If you dream about a large, powerful animal in an open field, it could symbolize freedom and the power to take control of your life. On the other hand, if it is in a dark and narrow cave, it could represent feeling trapped and suppressed.

The number of animals can be telling as well. One animal in a dream could represent the self, while two or more could symbolize the various aspects of your personality and how they interact.

Another factor to consider is the animal's behavior. Is it friendly or hostile? Passive or aggressive? Tame or wild? An animal's behavior in a dream offers insight into your current mindset and attitude. For example, if you dream of a tiger peacefully lounging in the sun, this could indicate that you feel relaxed and content in your current situation. On the other hand, if you dream of a tiger snarling and attacking you, this may mean that something or someone is threatening you.

Dreaming of a fight between two animals can signify an internal struggle or conflict within ourselves. It could also represent two parts of your life that oppose each other and must be reconciled. Animals in harmony could indicate a sense of peace and balance within yourself.

In addition to the species and behavior of the animal, it is essential to consider the dreamer's personal history and relationship with that particular type of animal. For example, if a dreamer had a traumatic experience with a specific animal, that could play out in their dream. This is incredibly influential if the dreamer feels fear or intense emotion upon seeing the animal in their dream.

Dreams with animals provide a unique insight into the subconscious, as they often represent aspects of yourself that you may not have been aware of or had difficulty expressing. Animals in dreams can symbolize instinctive behavior, primal and untamed emotions, or the power to tap into your deepest desires. Paying attention to the animal's context, behavior, and personal history can help you better understand your inner self and the forces that shape your life.

Dreams about Plants

Dreams about plants and trees can also be highly symbolic, as they are often strongly associated with growth, life, fertility, and a connection to nature. They can represent the health of a relationship, your physical well-being, or signify spiritual transformation. In dreams, plants symbolize various emotions and experiences, from birth to death and growth to decay.

The type of plant that appears in your dream is essential, as each species has unique meanings. For example, dreaming of a lush and vibrant garden could represent abundance. On the other hand, if the plants are wilted or dead, this could indicate that something is lacking or stagnating.

Trees

Trees are potent symbols of growth, life, and nature. A dream featuring a tree suggests that a person is ready to move forward and reach for success. Trees also represent knowledge, growth, and stability that can help overcome difficult times.

Dreams of trees can also relate to one's personal life and symbolize a solid or close relationship with others. Trees can represent family members, friends, or even higher power. In dreams, trees may also be interpreted as symbols of fertility and abundance.

Some trees have deep spiritual and religious connotations, such as the Tree of Life from Christianity or the Bodhi Tree from Buddhism.

Cactus

Dreams of cacti can be associated with protection, independence, and power. Cacti also symbolize strength in the face of adversity. They can indicate that someone is struggling to cope with a problematic situation or survive a challenging period. Cacti dreams suggest that the dreamer is feeling isolated and alone.

Coconut Palm

Coconut palms are usually associated with knowledge, wisdom, and progress. In many cultures, the coconut palm is considered a symbol of abundance, fertility, and growth. Symbolically, they represent a sense of resilience and strength, as they can grow in even the most adverse conditions. In dream interpretations, dreaming of a coconut palm could signify transformation and progress. It represents spiritual growth, new beginnings, changes in your life, and increased knowledge.

White Birch Trees

White birch trees often represent good luck, success, and hope in dreams. They symbolize flexibility, resilience, strength, and overcoming obstacles. These trees represent the need to be more flexible in life and to stay focused on the goal despite any difficulties that may come your way.

White Oak

White Oak is a beautiful and majestic tree representing courage, strength, and longevity. This tree suggests perseverance, stability, and a sense of security in dreams. It is a symbol of good luck and long-term success, so if you see a White Oak in your dream, it could represent a positive and encouraging outlook.

White Oak is also associated with the will to overcome obstacles and take on new challenges. If you dream of a White Oak, it can remind you to have faith and remain strong in difficult times. This tree also represents wisdom, patience, and fertility.

Dreams of Flowers

Flowers are often viewed as symbols of beauty, purity, and love in dreams. Dreaming of flowers represents the start of something new or a blossoming of ideas and thoughts. A bouquet can symbolize the gathering of courage, love, and strength that you need in life. A single flower can be a sign of innocence and vulnerability or even a reminder to care for yourself.

Rose

Roses are perhaps the most popular flowers in the world and often represent love, beauty, strength, innocence, and joy. In dreams, roses can symbolize various things; they often represent your feelings in your waking lives. For instance, if you dream of red roses, they may express passionate love, while white roses in your dream can signify purity and innocence.

Lily

The lily is a symbol of innocence, beauty, and purity. In dreams, it represents a sense of peace, serenity, and a longing for something beautiful. Dreaming of a white lily symbolizes purity and innocence, while a yellow lily may signify a desire for joy and happiness.

Sunflower

The sunflower symbolizes joy, creativity, strength, and growth. Such dreams often represent these qualities and signify hope and positivity. It indicates that you are headed in the right direction and can achieve your goals. It is also a sign of faith and optimism, as the sunflower always turns its face to the sun. Sunflower dreams often signify that you are entering a season of prosperity and abundance.

Morning Glory

Morning glory dreams are believed to be connected with new beginnings and fresh starts. It can symbolize the start of a new journey in life or a new project. Dreaming of these flowers often represents the potential for growth, fertility, and a strong connection to nature. They are also associated with the ability to heal oneself and others.

Tulip

Tulips are a sign of creativity and freedom.[18]

Tulips are a popular and beautiful flower known for their bright colors, long stems, and simple petals. In dream interpretation, tulips are seen as a sign of beauty, freedom, and creativity. They often show up when you need to express yourself or open up to new ideas. When you dream of a tulip, it may signify that you need to look at things with fresh eyes and find inspiration in something new.

Plants and animals are common habitants of your dreamscape, and they often appear in symbolic form to give you important messages about your waking life. In addition to general symbolism, each type of plant or animal can have a special meaning when it appears in your dream. Taking the time to examine and interpret these symbols can be a helpful tool for understanding your subconscious and gaining insight into your life. However, remember that dream interpretation is personal, and the meaning of these animals and plants differs from person to person. It is best to explore the symbolism of a dream in the context of your own life and experiences.

Chapter 8: Dreams about Body Parts

Dreams are an incredible yet intricate phenomenon that holds an infinite array of symbolism and meanings. Dreams containing body parts, in particular, can be especially confusing as they can have many different connotations and layers of interpretations. While some may represent things like physical health or developmental growth, others refer to feelings and emotions within yourself or interactions with those around you. Inevitably, unlocking the true meaning behind these dreams can sometimes be a difficult task. This chapter sheds light on the confusion of dreams about body parts. Through exploring the symbolism, one can better understand why their dream is present and what it is trying to tell them about their life and current situation.

Hair

Hair is a common dream symbol, and the meaning changes depending on its context. Dreaming of styled hair might represent vanity, while a haircut in a dream could symbolize a new start or phase in your life. Unruly or chaotic hair often reflects feeling overwhelmed and out of control, while clean and neat hair indicates feelings of contentment and stability. Generally, long hair is associated with femininity and youthfulness, while short hair suggests strength and maturity. Hair can also mean spiritual or creative energy when seen intertwined with vines or other natural elements; this type of dream may suggest you need to express yourself creatively or re-establish a connection to nature.

Head

Dreams involving the head tend to symbolize your intellectual ability and how you process the events in your life. For example, a dream about having a large head could symbolize feeling "headstrong" and thinking you know better than anyone else. In contrast, if you dream of having a small head, it could mean you're overly humble or feel inadequate. Dreams about an injured or diseased head can symbolize mental distress or an inability to process your current reality. These dream symbols provide insight into your subconscious mind and offer valuable clues about yourself.

Brain

Dreams about brains often symbolize your power of thought and intellect. They are a sign that your mind is trying to process and contain a large amount of information. The symbolism can have a range of themes depending on the context; if a dream involves emotions, for example, it might suggest that the dreamer is subconsciously working through feelings or conflicts within themselves. Alternatively, if the dream mainly revolved around problem-solving tasks, it could indicate the dreamer is feeling pressure to find solutions to life dilemmas. Thus, when dreaming about brains, consider the other symbols associated with their presence to interpret the real deep-seated meaning of such dreams.

Nose

Dream symbolism of the nose reflects a "sense" you have for a certain situation—which can take many forms. For example, if you dream that someone has a large, prominent nose, it could signify they are aware of what is happening around them. On the flip side, dreaming of an absent or non-existent nose can suggest someone is not paying attention to their environment or trying to avoid responsibility. It's also been said that the size of the nose in your dream could correspond to how much effort you're putting into something—with a larger, more prominent nose representing more effort than a smaller one.

Teeth

Teeth are a common symbol dreamt of by people all over the world, with various interpretations as to what they mean. Dreams involving teeth often symbolize anxieties and fears, representing how these fears feel; sharp and painful. Teeth can represent power or control; if someone is portrayed as having vicious, razor-sharp teeth, it could represent fear of that person's influence. One could also dream about budding teeth in childhood, representing growing mental responsibilities with age. These teeth might even foreshadow future successes or failures in life. Alongside this, teeth represent communication, or having issues with your teeth in dreams can mean you're having difficulty making yourself heard or getting your message across. If a person has to have their teeth treated in the dreamscape, it can signify overpowering emotions that need tending to. Ultimately, dreaming about teeth can have numerous meanings depending on the context, so paying attention to details while interpreting such dreams is important.

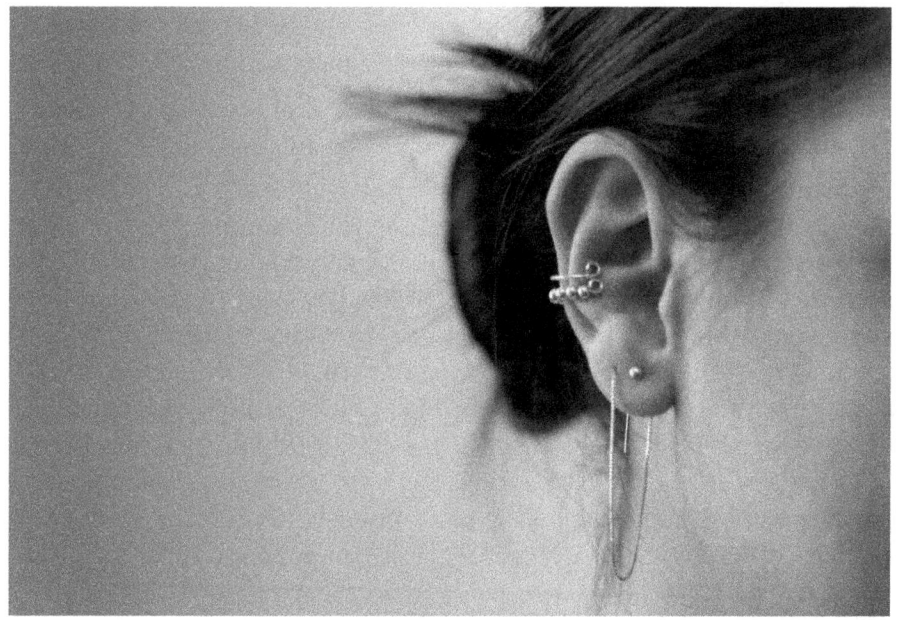

Ears have different meanings in a dream depending on the context.[14]

Dreaming about ears can mean various things depending on the context. From spiritual to physical senses, dreaming of ears indicates that you are listening to something or someone. Ears in a dream often represent a person's ability to trust and be trusted. Symbols of objective perception, ears can suggest that an individual is paying attention, seeking knowledge, and being open-minded. In some cases, dreaming of ears also signifies obstacles blocking communication with others and deceit from someone close to you or even yourself. For example, if your ear is blocked or clogged, it may mean inner turmoil, or you're overwhelmed with thoughts and opinions that do not align with your beliefs. Ultimately, dreaming about ears conveys the overall of listening carefully with intention and discernment.

Back

Dreams featuring backs signify the different layers of protection and support you have in your life. A back symbolizes strength and security, so a dream about having a strong and solid back can represent emotional stability and a newfound belief in your trustworthiness. On the other hand, if you dream of having an injured or weak back, this may signify feelings of vulnerability or insecurity. Additionally, a dream about someone else's back can suggest that you're over-reliant on them for safety and comfort, which may be negatively impacting your emotional well-being. More broadly, dreams featuring backs suggest something hidden or something hidden within you that needs protecting, and you need to strengthen those areas before moving forward in your life.

Tongue

Dreams involving tongues can have many meanings; however, they generally relate to communication or miscommunication. A dream where you are speaking with an uncontrollable tongue might symbolize feelings that the speaker is not being heard, while dreaming of someone else's tongue could represent the feeling that the dreamer is completely outside of a conversation. Likewise, seeing an abnormally long tongue can indicate having difficulty conveying your thoughts to others. Saying something with a tongue made up of food could show dissatisfaction and suggest your words are not being taken seriously. An unmovable tongue might reveal feeling powerless and unable to express opinions, warn others, or simply be heard by those around you. All these can be seen as indications of anxiety around communication.

Breasts

One of the most common dream symbols, breasts are often associated with nourishment, femininity, and fertility. The symbolism of breasts can indicate a need for comfort and nurture in waking life in both males and females. Breasts may carry overtones related to maternal protection when viewed as a nurturing entity, while the sexuality of breasts can also be represented in dreams to symbolize lustful desires or a sense of connectedness. In general, dreaming of breasts represents physical or emotional nourishment, deeply embedded spiritual connections, and the possibility of motherhood. While these are some core ideas around breast symbolism, each dreamer's experience will ultimately be based on personal interpretation determined by current life circumstances.

Nipples

Dreaming about nipples may indicate that you seek ways to connect with another person, either intimately or generally. It could also symbolize a desire for nourishment and comfort and a search for emotional sustenance. Additionally, dreaming of nipples forms part of sexual themes as they are connected to one's most intimate parts, where feelings of desire are produced and explored in dream-states. By understanding the different concepts connected with dreaming of nipples, people can understand their unconscious desires better and get new insights into their lives.

Arms

Arms represent strength, power, aggression, and protection. Sometimes dreams of arms represent feelings of being armed with abilities or resources to handle life's tasks and challenges. They may symbolize the ability to reach out for help or for someone to reach out and offer assistance. Other times, dreams about arms may indicate a need for self-defense or an effort to defend a loved one against danger.

Abdomen

Abdomen dream symbolism is quite fascinating and has a multitude of meanings. Generally, the abdomen is associated with self-control, emotions, financial stability, and issues of fertility or infertility. When dreaming about your abdomen, it could indicate that something you have inside you needs attention and release. It could be a reminder to focus on maintaining balance in your life and controlling any extreme emotions that may be ruling your behavior. Alternatively, it could symbolize the structure of one's identity or a need for financial freedom to feel secure. Abdominal pain or wounds in the dream world can indicate infertility issues, while sculpted abs can represent strength and power. Dream symbols about the abdomen are powerful indicators that healing needs to occur to restore harmony in one's life.

Fingers

Dreaming about fingers has a lot of symbolism, depending on context. Generally, fingers represent assertiveness and strength. However, if the fingers in your dream are broken or mutilated, this may represent feelings of helplessness. If you find yourself counting your fingers in the dream-state, this could suggest that you are feeling overwhelmed by daily responsibilities and tasks. Dreaming of shaking hands with someone else can often signify a connection between two parties—it generally represents understanding and respect for each other's opinions. On the other hand, if you're clenching your fist in the dream, you might feel angry or frustrated—and perhaps you lack control over something occurring in your life. Understanding different symbolic fingers can reveal what is happening in your mind and is quite fascinating.

Palm

If a dream features a person holding their right palm open toward you, it is often interpreted as a sign of reconciliation or friendship. When featured in dreamscapes with loved ones, clutching someone's hand could represent their comforting presence and protection against life's difficulties. Seeing the palm of your hand in a dream often symbolizes hope or trust that you are beginning to have in yourself—like having faith to find the courage to start something new or overcome obstacles. It could also be a reminder that you possess the strength to confront fearful situations or take on ambitious endeavors. Consequently, dreams featuring palms of hands can mean many things, from protectiveness to hope—a universal symbol with various themes and interpretations.

Genitals

Dreams involving genitals are surprisingly common and can often carry deep psychological messages. Generally, having genital dreams means the dreamer is transitioning in some way, exploring a new identity, or embracing an existing one. It may also signify the opportunity to make a powerful shift in perspective, allowing you to take ownership of your life. For some people, it represents a sexual desire or the integration of their gender identity. Additionally, dreams that focus on genitals can symbolize how someone experiences themselves on the most intimate level, highlighting both positive and negative elements of their self-image. Overall, dreams featuring your sexual organs provide insight into how you navigate power dynamics within yourself and in your relationships.

Buttocks

The buttocks are a prominent dream symbol representing sensuality, fertility, and physical power. Dreams often reflect the need for dreamers to express themselves or move freely. This can be interpreted as a search for passion and independence from external expectations. The buttocks have also been linked to growth and exploration in different aspects of life, such as career goals, relationships, and self-reflection. Symbolically, the buttocks may suggest that you are working toward coming into your own power and embracing yourself fully.

Ankles

Ankles have long been a symbol with several different layers of meaning. In some cultures, ankles represent stability and home—feeling secure and rooted in your life. A dream in which ankles are prominent may represent a need to focus on making plans or forming strong foundations for yourself. Ankles can stand for sensuality and femininity. A dream involving ankle-bearing clothes could reveal that you are exploring your sex appeal, while ankle imagery around heights may suggest being held back by feelings of self-doubt or insecurity about the future. While the symbolism for ankles varies from culture to culture, it is undeniable that these flexible joints conjure up powerful emotions—both positive and negative—no matter where you come from.

Knees

Dreaming about knees is a particularly unique and fascinating topic. The symbolic meanings behind knee-related dreams vary greatly depending on what appears in the dream. Generally, dreaming about knees represents flexibility, vulnerability, or stability. For example, if a person's knees are strong and stable in the dreamscape, this could symbolize self-confidence and resilience. Alternatively, if the knees appear weak and fragile in the dream, it can suggest feelings of instability or weakening resolve regarding an issue or situation. Similarly, if a person can move their body parts with ease in the dream—from bending down to crouching—this may allude to one's level of flexibility in life or your ability to think outside of the box quickly and effectively. Altogether, these interpretations are valuable insights for interpreting knee symbolism within dreams.

Legs

Dreams, filled with symbolism, can uncover your subconscious thoughts and emotions, so the meaning of some bizarre elements may have particular significance. One commonly experienced dream symbol is legs. Generally, dreaming about legs can represent your desire for stability and balance or indicate how you approach a certain situation by either walking away from it or stepping forward. It may also point to feeling bound or restricted in life, struggling to move ahead, or trapped without an escape. In addition, dreams about legs may imply confidence and strength or symbolize overcoming obstacles regardless of size. Alternatively, dreaming about arachnoid legs could symbolize difficult moments that will soon pass if you remain resourceful. Leg dreams are often highly individualized and can depend on the feelings the dreamer associates with them to get an accurate interpretation—so think carefully before coming to any conclusions.

Toes

Dreaming about toes can be puzzling, but it actually says quite a lot about your current state of mind and emotions. Toes often symbolize balance in your life; if your toes are healthy and you can walk without difficulty, it may mean that you are feeling balanced in every aspect of your life or that you're feeling hopeful. However, if the toes appear broken or unhealthy, it likely means someone is feeling out of control. Additionally, dreaming about any type of movement involving toes, such as running or dancing, could represent joy and happiness, while dreaming about step-counting suggests focusing on details or avoiding trouble. Overall, the dream symbolism of toes ranges from feelings of accomplishment to hopelessness, depending on the dreamer's current situation.

Blood

Blood is a powerful symbol that has been used to represent a variety of themes throughout history and across cultures. Historically, it has often been associated with life and death and pain or suffering—reflecting its position between the two states. It can also represent intense emotions like anger, violence, and passion. In dream symbolism, blood may be interpreted differently depending on the context in which it appears. Sometimes it may signify loss or sadness, but it can also signal protection or healing. On an even deeper level, blood in a dream might point toward ancestral memory, soul loss, and even spiritual transformation. Whatever form its presence takes, blood dreams are thought to have unique significance as they often reflect intense internal struggles of one's subconscious nature.

Bones

Bones are a common symbol in dreams, representing both life and death. Dreams featuring bones can often represent something that has died or a cycle that has been broken, such as the breaking of an old habit or attitude. On the other hand, they can symbolize strength, resilience, and ancestors who have passed on their wisdom and knowledge. For example, dreaming of an old ancient skeleton may represent a connection to your past and how it influences your life today. Additionally, dreaming of multiple or incomplete bones may indicate a feeling of being incomplete on some level, with certain areas of your life needing attention.

All in all, bones are powerful symbols filled with deep meaning that capture the fragility and beauty of life.

Chapter 9: When Supernatural Beings Appear

Your subconscious generates dreams. This part of your mind is responsible for imagination, intuition, and hidden desires and values. Besides images of yourself and regular beings, your imagination can also create supernatural characters or beings. Dragons, angels, spirits, sprites, and dwarves are just some of the common characters that might appear in people's dreams. This chapter explores the meaning of these supernatural characters appearing in dreams, analyzing the symbolism and variations.

Dreams about Angels

Dreaming of angels is a positive sign. Angels can offer wisdom, protection, guidance, assurance, and purification. In many cultures, angels are also considered messengers of the gods; however, they can have other functions, too. Some angels specialize in specific spiritual matters, and they will provide their assistance in that field. Guardian angels have a powerful connection to their charge and stay with them for most of their lives. Other angels simply materialize because they were available at that time and noticed their help was required.

Whichever type of angel appears in your dreams, they'll likely come in the same way each time. They can appear on a sign, fly, talk, or sing to your dream reality. Angels can also emerge in more subtly forms, including:

- Rainbows in the sky
- Other angelic symbols in the sky
- White feathers around you
- Feeling nurturing energy around you
- A sudden flash of light
- A voice that seemingly comes from nowhere
- The feeling of an invisible hand touching you
- Tingling sensation on your body or head

If an angel appears in your dreams (whether in person or through symbols) and you notice that you're feeling happy when you wake up, you have been blessed with their energy. It could also signify that you've needed reassurance for an upcoming challenge or advice for overcoming toxic influences.

If an angel is singing or talking to you in your dreams, they're opening your soul for their wisdom. It helps to share your grievances and worries so they can understand you better. This dream symbolizes your triumph over a past hurt or upcoming challenge. It can act as a form of intervention—in case you know that you need reassurance or advice. Whether the angel's words sound familiar to you or not, do not worry. They carry an eternal blessing your soul will understand and embrace without words. If you remember an angel talking to you but cannot recall their words, try to bring them back in bits and pieces through meditation. Your conversation will likely be stored in your subconscious. You just need the right tool to access it. When you do, you'll know in which direction to move forward.

Angels and demons often appear together and interact in dreams. If you see them fighting, this indicates that you're experiencing an inner conflict. It's most likely about right or wrong decisions or heading in the right direction. Maybe something is holding you back from moving toward a better path. This hindrance can be represented by the two opposing forces in your dream. The inner struggle can also stem from negative emotions, addictions, powerful urges, or similar self-limiting behavior.

The dreams will go away after acknowledging your conflict, focusing on surrounding yourself with good energies, and fighting off the toxic influences that cause the dispute. If they don't, you still have issues to work through.

If you dream of angel wings, you're protected by a powerful energy. If you focus hard enough, you'll feel this energy surrounding you. This dream will likely appear when you're going through a challenging period and need added protection.

While grown angels appear prevalently in dreams, some people also dream of baby angels of cherubs. If you notice an innocent-looking baby angel suddenly appear in your dreams, you're being offered extensive protection from above. These beings have many heavenly roles, including protecting the entrance to the Garden of Eden, which speaks of their closeness with God and the other angels. If you dream of a baby angel, you'll face a sudden major hurdle in life and need any angelic help you can get to overcome your challenges.

Dreams about Demons

Demons in dreams are never a good sign. These beings are linked to hostile forces. If they appear in your dreams, you have every reason to be alarmed. You are likely being affected by negative energies in your waking life. These energies can have detrimental consequences for your life. It could be an unpleasant work situation or relationship with a boss or colleague, bringing you down and blocking your professional development. Or, it can represent a place where you would feel safe but have to spend many hours—resulting in anxiety and other imbalances between the different parts of your life. Demons can also be linked to complex real-life individuals who secretly want you to fail. These complex individuals hide their true (demonic) face very well. You must be careful about interacting with such people to reveal who they are.

Dreams about Dragons

Dreaming about dragons has several meanings. The particular circumstances, the color and shape of the dragon, and their behavior all affect the meaning of this dream. In ancient Western cultures, dragons were often viewed as adversaries that warriors needed to defeat to secure their community. Because of this, many view "dream dragons" as harbingers of problems, destruction, and suffering in real life. Angry dragons also denote negative sentiments and behavior, typically born of anger and loss of control.

That said, in Eastern cultures, dragons have a very different image. They are thought to bring good luck, protection, and balance into people's lives. If you dream of a magnificent, colorful wingless dragon that acts friendly, it could be that you're yearning for freedom and balance. If it's a recurring dream, you're on your way to establishing this balance.

Dragons in dreams can symbolize power, authority figures, or your desire to have these characteristics. Dragons are also known to be eccentric. Dreaming about them can indicate that you have a passionate personality and are prone to finding unorthodox solutions for your problems. Or, you may have a hidden desire to express your passion, seek out new adventures, or regret missing opportunities to have funds in the past.

While dreaming about angry dragons can be scary, remember that these creatures often hint at your pent-up subconscious emotions and repressed thoughts. It can further imply an issue or conflict with another person in your work or personal life.

Dreams about Dwarves

If you see a dwarf in your dream, you are lucky. These unusual creatures are symbols of good fortune and surprises. It could mean you will win the lottery and have enough money not to worry about your finances for a while. Or, you might receive an inheritance or an unexpectedly good return on investment. If there are several dwarves in your dreams and you know that you'll be playing the lottery, this suggests that you should share your ticket with others so that they can take part in your good luck.

Dreams about Spirits

Dream images of spirits are probably the most common in dreams of supernatural beings. Nearly all ancient cultures have myths and records about spirits. Knowing this, it is not surprising that these creatures made their way into the imagination responsible for dream aspects. Most cultures agree that spirits can be ambivalent in nature. They can appear as visions, voices, or symbols in dreams, providing guidance, healing, and protection or, in some cases, causing disruption.

The meanings of spirit dreams can vary depending on the circumstances and actions of these entities in the dream world. Some believe that vivid dreams about spirits—particularly the spirit of your loved ones—indicate a strong connection and the actual appearance of the soul in your dreams. Dreaming about fictional spirits is just your brain's way of processing information related to your thoughts and emotions.

In most cases, dreaming of spirits indicates that you have unfinished business in your waking life. This association stems from the common belief that spirits that come back to visit also have unresolved issues in this world. Besides this, spirit dreams can denote uncertainty and uncoordinated thought processes. You may be at a crossroads in life and unsure where to go next. Or, maybe you're just curious about where life leads you but cannot help feeling nervous about it. Due to their ethereal nature, dreaming about spirits may be about you feeling invisible in your personal or professional life.

Spirits in dreams are a comforting phenomenon because they represent life after death. However, they can be seen as signs of mortality. For example, if you aren't taking care of yourself, dreaming about spirits can be a warning that you should start paying more attention to your health.

Spirits can also be seen as reflections of your hidden side, the part you aren't comfortable with and don't want to confront. For example, if you dream about a spirit you can't see, just feel and notice the signs they're sending you. Consider doing some introspection to see what you're trying to hide about yourself. There might be something you pretend not to see, but your subconscious will still sense it.

Spirits rarely speak to you directly in your dreams, but they might do other things. If the spirits in your dreams are moving items around you, this could indicate that you lack control of some areas of your waking life.

The appearance of spirits in your dream can be a stressful experience. If you feel haunted by the spirit or suffocated by its negative energy, this indicates that you feel overwhelmed by people or situations in the real world. You might also fear the unknown, so you stick to familiar waters, even if this hinders your progress and growth. If you're someone who often worries about the future, you're likely to have this dream. No matter how insignificant the event is, you can't help but expect the worst possible outcome. Constantly thinking that something untoward will happen soon will make you worried and project your thoughts and emotions into your subconscious. Haunting spirits further signify a vulnerable emotional state. If you feel negative about someone or something in your waking life, now is the time to deal with them so that you can regain control of your feelings.

If you dream about being a ghost, it could mean that you are experiencing extreme guilt about past events. Maybe you've hurt someone intentionally and never had the chance to say sorry or rectify the situation.

Confronting your guilt can help you overcome it. Some people also have a paralyzing fear of spirits in their dreams. Again, this is fear from real life projected into your dream world. You'll need to look around for its cause and overcome your fear by taking a more positive approach to the situation.

If you dream about the spirits of loved ones who have passed away, the dream is about your connection with them. You might need to have a final talk with them to find closure. They might need reassurance that everything will be all right and that you've accepted their passing and moved on with your life.

Dreams about Sprites

Dreaming about sprites reflects your hope and confidence in your abilities to reach your goals. Just like angels, fairies in dreams are also good omens. Fairies usually seem like friendly creatures, so dreaming about them is associated with happiness. You may earn a significant achievement in life or obtain something you have desperately missed or thought impossible to achieve. Or, you may have found an item or connection you have lost.

While dreams about sprites rarely have negative connotations, you should still be careful. There are malicious fairies that are anything but friendly and helpful. If you dream of a mischievous fairy, this indicates that your emotional life is out of balance. If you feel scared of the spirits in your dreams, this could signify that you have issues in one of your relationships. Maybe someone wants to be a part of your life, even if you do not wish to have any connections with them.

Dreaming of a fairy wand is a message full of wisdom. It often means that you should listen to people around you when making important decisions, as they will have some wise suggestions. This particularly applies if you want to make a profit on something. Sprites can give you plenty of financial gains—you'll just have to listen to their advice.

Vampires in dreams symbolize your energy being drained in waking life.[15]

Dreams about Vampires

Vampires are known to feed on the blood of living people. If they appear in your dreams, it could mean that something or someone is draining your energy in your waking life. Blood symbolizes the energy that sustains your mind, body, and soul—something you cannot survive without. Dreaming about vampires is a warning for you to look closely at your environment and identify which parts are sucking the life out of you. Think about the areas of your life in which you have difficulty moving forward, or feel that you are not doing a good enough job. Maybe your employer is setting unreasonable deadlines for your projects, causing you to fail to finish them. Or, you might have a controlling partner who does not let you express your personality and needs in your relationships. You can just as well have a friend constantly complaining about something, bringing you down with their negativity and taking your time away from more productive pursuits.

Spirit Guides

Most spirit guides are souls residing in the spiritual realm. Instead of moving on to another life cycle, they have chosen to remain and watch over their living descendants. These are the souls of the ancestors, recently passed loved ones or pets, or people you've looked up to during their life. However, spirit guides can also be supernatural beings, including fairies, angels, and demons.

You are paired with a spirit guide who can best serve you in any situation. This can mean that you will have several spirit guides at a time. For example, if you're in a tough situation, you may need the complementary strengths and wisdom of an ancestor and an angel. The ancestor will provide you with the knowledge you need to find a solution, while the angel will empower you with their guidance.

Your spirit guides know you better than you know yourself, which makes them helpful in spiritual growth and healing. This is also why they will not appear in the form you would expect them to. Most people are unaware of their spirit guides being around because they appear in unique forms—like patterns in a dream, for example. If you see a character trying to guide you through your dreams, this is a common sign of a spiritual companion being at work. They may point to a specific place in the dream world, tell you to follow them, or show you a symbol representing the next step you need to take.

Some guides only appear for a short time, help you through a particularly difficult time, and then leave once your issues have been resolved. Let's say you have had a recurring dream about a supernatural being, but it stopped. This could have been a spiritual companion that has fulfilled their purpose. Other guides are there to assist you in your relationship, experiences, business deals, or events; however, when these end, the entities will move on, too.

Other companions are like experts in their field (like archangels) and appear and disappear as needed. Some guides are just there to help you overcome your loss. For example, if you dream about a pet you've lost recently, it might be their soul telling you that it's time to move on. Most people have one or more lifetime guises. You meet these souls in childhood, and they'll stay with you for the rest of your life. They appear in dreams, visions, and symbols in your environment. They help you uncover your gifts, guide you toward the right path, and help you stay on your chosen path. Spiritual companions can take the shape of any animal, plant, or supernatural being. If you have recurrent dreams about a specific supernatural entity, animal, or plant, this could be your spirit guide's way of trying to establish contact. Your guides can be persistent, especially when they know you need them. There are many reasons why your spirit guides will not appear in their original form. For example, many people cannot handle seeing a spiritual guide's true face. If your guardian thinks you aren't ready, they'll only send you subtle signals and appear in other forms until you've bonded with them and are ready to accept their true nature. Different entities have different abilities. Your spirit guide might not appear in front of you in your dreams because they simply can't.

Chapter 10: Advanced Dream Interpretation Techniques

Dreams can be filled with strange, mysterious characters and symbols that seem to have no real-world equivalent. They are a reflection of the subconscious mind, and as such, they can reveal hidden thoughts, emotions, and desires that you may be unaware of in your waking life. However, dreams can be difficult to understand, as they are filled with symbols that can seem confusing or meaningless. While some people believe that dreams have a universal meaning that can be easily deciphered, the truth is that the interpretation of dreams is a highly personal and subjective process.

One of the limitations of dream interpretation is the idea that there is a universal meaning behind dream symbols. For instance, some people believe that a dream about a snake always represents danger or temptation; however, the truth is that the interpretation of a dream symbol is unique to the dreamer. In fact, the same symbol can have different meanings for different people, depending on their personal associations and cultural background.

This chapter focuses on the importance of personal associations, emotions, and context in dream analysis. By exploring how you feel during the dream, focusing on the characters and objects that stand out to you, and considering the context of the dream, you can gain a deeper understanding of what your dream may be trying to tell you.

Asking the Right Questions

Recalling a dream can be a daunting task, especially if the dream seems fragmented or confusing. Fortunately, by using the 5Ws technique, you can start to piece together the details of your dream and make sense of what happened. Once you have a basic understanding of the details of your dream, it is time to use the answers to guide the interpretation process.

Who were the characters in your dream, and what roles did they play? What objects or symbols stood out to you, and why? Where did the dream take place, and what was the significance of the location? When did the dream occur, and what events led up to it? By answering these questions, you can start to uncover the hidden messages and meanings in your dream.

It's also important to explore any significant events, emotions, or thoughts from the previous day that may have influenced your dream. Dreams are often a reflection of your subconscious thoughts and emotions, so it's possible that something from your waking life may have triggered the dream. Perhaps you had a stressful day at work, or maybe you had an important conversation with a loved one. As you work through the interpretation process, pay close attention to your emotions and feelings during the dream. Did you feel scared, anxious, or overwhelmed? Or did you feel happy, loved, or content? The emotions you experience during the dream can offer important clues to the underlying messages and meanings.

Here is an example you can consider for learning how to interpret your dreams better:

Let's say that you dreamt you were at a party with your friends. Here's how you could use the 5Ws to analyze the dream:

- **Who?** Who was at the party with you? Were they people you know in real life, or were they strangers?
- **What?** What happened at the party? Did you have fun, or did something go wrong? Were there any objects or symbols that stood out to you?
- **When?** When did the dream occur? Was it during the day or at night? Did anything happen before the dream that might have influenced it?

- **Where?** Where was the party held? Was it a familiar location or somewhere new?
- **Why?** Why were you at the party? Did you have a specific goal or objective, or were you just there to have fun?

Let's say that upon reflection, you realize the people at the party were your high school friends who you haven't seen in years. You had a great time at the party, but you remember feeling a bit out of place. You also noticed that there was a clock on the wall that kept ticking faster and faster. Using this information, you can start to explore the underlying messages and meanings in your dream. Perhaps the dream represents a desire to reconnect with old friends but also a fear of feeling out of place or not fitting in. The ticking clock could symbolize a sense of urgency or the feeling that time is running out. Alternatively, it could represent a fear of missing out on opportunities or not making the most of your time.

By exploring these ideas and paying attention to your emotions during the dream, you can start to uncover the hidden messages and meanings in your dream and gain a deeper understanding of yourself and your subconscious mind.

Emotions are important to consider when interpreting dreams.[16]

Examining Emotions and Feelings

Emotions are a crucial element to consider when it comes to dreaming interpretation. Dreams often tap into your deepest feelings and emotions—how you feel during the dream and when you wake can give some important insights into what the dream might be trying to tell you. So, you must consider your emotions during the dream to analyze them effectively. Were you feeling anxious, scared, or overwhelmed? Or were you feeling calm, joyful, or curious? These emotions can offer significant clues as to the meaning of the dream. For example, feeling afraid of a character in the dream may indicate a sense of vulnerability or insecurity, while feeling comforted by that same character might indicate a need for support or guidance. When you woke up, did you feel relieved to wake up from a scary dream? Or did you feel sad to leave a pleasant dream behind? These emotions can provide further insights into the underlying messages and meanings of the dream.

When interpreting dream symbols or characters, consider the emotions associated with them. For example, a dream about a snake might evoke feelings of fear or disgust for some people, while others might feel fascinated or intrigued. These emotional responses can influence how the snake is interpreted in the dream. Similarly, a dream about a loved one may have very different meanings depending on whether the dreamer felt happy, sad, or conflicted in the dream. Emotions can offer important clues as to what the dream is trying to communicate and help you unlock hidden messages and meanings. Consider these examples to understand how emotions play into the interpretation of a dream:

- **A dream about flying:** If the dreamer feels joyful and free while flying, this could symbolize a sense of liberation or the ability to rise above challenges in their waking life. However, if the dreamer feels anxious or scared while flying, this could symbolize a fear of failure or loss of control.

- **A dream about water:** If the dreamer feels calm and peaceful while swimming in a body of water, this could symbolize emotional balance and tranquility. However, if the dreamer feels overwhelmed or anxious while navigating choppy waters, this could indicate a sense of being overwhelmed by emotions or life's challenges.

- **A dream about a house:** If the dreamer feels happy and comfortable in the house, this could symbolize a sense of security and belonging. However, if the dreamer feels uneasy or scared while exploring the house, this could indicate a fear of the unknown or feeling lost in their waking life.

- **A dream about a loved one:** If the dreamer feels happy and loved while interacting with a loved one in the dream, this could symbolize a deep connection and sense of support. However, if the dreamer feels conflicted or upset while interacting with the loved one, this could indicate unresolved issues or a need for closure.

- **A dream about a car:** If the dreamer feels in control and confident while driving a car, this could symbolize independence and self-determination. However, if the dreamer feels out of control or anxious while driving the car, this could indicate a fear of losing control or a need for guidance in their waking life.

Using Creative Interpretation Techniques

By approaching dream analysis with an open mind and a willingness to explore different perspectives, you can uncover hidden symbols, associations, and connections that might not be immediately apparent. Creative interpretation techniques involve thinking outside the box and considering multiple possibilities for what a symbol or character might represent. They encourage you to trust your instincts and draw upon your experiences and personal associations when interpreting your dreams. In the following sections, several advanced dream analysis techniques will be explored.

1. Amplification

This technique involves expanding on the images and symbols in your dream by exploring their historical, cultural, and personal associations. It involves exploring the rich web of associations and meanings surrounding a dream symbol or image. This technique is based on the idea that a dream image can have many layers of meaning and that by delving deeper into these meanings, you can better understand the message behind the dream.

To use the amplification technique, you start by identifying a symbol or image that stood out to you in the dream. Then consider all the possible meanings and associations that come to mind when you think of that symbol. This could involve drawing on personal experiences, cultural symbols, historical references, and other sources of inspiration. By exploring these associations and amplifying the symbol's meaning, you can uncover new insights into the dream and its significance.

For example, let's say you had a dream about a cat. Using the amplification technique, you can start by considering all of the possible meanings and associations of a cat. Consider the cat's physical characteristics, such as agility, independence, and grace. Also, consider cultural associations with cats, such as their role in ancient Egyptian mythology as protectors of the afterlife. Finally, reflect on your experiences with cats, including any positive or negative emotions you associate with these animals. You may realize that the cat symbolizes your desire for independence and freedom or represents a sense of mystery and intrigue in your waking life.

2. Active Imagination

An active imagination is a powerful dream analysis technique involving engaging with your dream's symbols and images through visualization and active participation. With an active imagination, you do not just observe your dream images; you immerse yourself in them and explore their full range of meanings and associations. To use active imagination, start by identifying a symbol or image that stood out to you in your dream. Then, try to visualize yourself interacting with that symbol or image, using all your senses to immerse yourself into the dream world fully. Imagine yourself talking to a dream character, exploring a dream landscape, or participating in a dream event.

Let's say you had a dream in which you were walking through a dark alleyway. You felt scared and vulnerable in the dream, and shadowy figures lurked in the corners. When you woke up, you still felt a sense of fear and unease, and you were not sure what the dream might be trying to tell you. To use active imagination to analyze this dream, you might start by visualizing yourself back in the dream, walking through the alleyway once again. As you walk, try to pay attention to the details of your environment: What do you see, hear, and feel? Are there any particular sensations or emotions that stand out to you?

Next, you could try to interact with the dream environment in some way. For example, you might try to find a way out of the alleyway or confront the shadowy figures lurking there. As you interact with the dream, pay attention to how your emotions and thoughts are changing. Do you feel more or less afraid? Are you experiencing any sense of empowerment or control? As you continue to engage with the dream in your visualization, you may uncover new insights and associations. For example, you may realize that the dream represents a fear or anxiety you have been struggling with in your waking life. Or, you might discover that the dream is pointing you toward a situation or relationship that feels unsafe or threatening.

3. Dialogue

The dialogue technique is a powerful tool for dream interpretation, as it allows you to explore the relationships and interactions between different elements of your dream in a more nuanced and dynamic way. Rather than simply analyzing each element independently, you can use dialogue to create a more complex and layered understanding of the dream as a whole. To use the dialogue technique, start by identifying two or more elements of your dream that seem to be in conflict or conversation with each other.

Let's say you have a dream in which you are standing on a beach, looking out at the ocean. As you watch the waves, you notice a small boat in the distance heading toward you. As the boat gets closer, you see it is piloted by a figure you cannot quite make out. As the boat pulls up to the shore, you realize that the pilot is actually your father, who passed away several years ago. He invites you onto the boat and begins to steer it out into the open ocean. As you're sailing together, you feel a mix of emotions—excitement, joy, and a sense of deep sadness at the same time.

To use the dialogue technique to interpret this dream, imagine a conversation between yourself and your father on the boat. What would you say to him, and what would he say to you? What emotions would you express, and how would he respond? As you imagine this dialogue, you will uncover new insights and associations about your relationship with your father and your emotions and desires. For example, you might realize that the dream is tapping into your longing for connection and intimacy with your father or that the boat represents a journey or transition you're currently going through.

4. Gestalt

The Gestalt technique is another great tool for dream interpretation to help you uncover deeper insights into the patterns and themes that underlie your dreams. To use this technique, you will need to approach your dream with an open mind and a willingness to explore its various elements and relationships. For example, let's say that you dream of walking through a crowded marketplace, browsing the stalls, and chatting with vendors. As you're walking, you notice a recurring pattern of red and green colors, which seem to appear in different forms throughout the dream—from the fruit and vegetables at the stalls to the clothing of the people around you.

To use the Gestalt technique to interpret this dream, try to look at the dream as a whole and explore the relationships and connections between the different elements. What do the red and green colors represent to you, and how do they relate to the other elements of the dream? What patterns and themes emerge when you look at the dream as a whole? You might realize that the red and green colors represent different sides of your emotional life—with red representing passion and intensity and green representing growth and abundance. Or you might see the crowded marketplace as a symbol of your desire for connection and social interaction, and the recurring colors highlight the different emotional experiences you encounter in these situations.

These advanced interpretation techniques can help you better understand your dreams and uncover hidden messages and meanings that you might have missed with a more basic analysis. However, keep in mind that dream interpretation is subjective, and there is no one "right" way to interpret a dream. The key is to stay open-minded, explore different possibilities, and trust your intuition. Do not be afraid to experiment with different approaches and techniques until you find what works best. Trust your intuition and allow yourself to be guided by your insights and inner wisdom.

Glossary of Dream Symbols

Colors

Black: Black suggests feelings of sadness or despair in a dream; however, it can also reflect power and strength. It may further represent obstacles that need to be overcome.

Blue: Blues are usually associated with feelings of peace and tranquility in dreams. They may also signify spiritual guidance or positive communication.

Brown: Brown points to feelings of stability, reliability, and comfort. It can also indicate a need to be grounded in reality.

Gold: Gold generally symbolizes wealth and riches in dreams but can also represent wisdom and spiritual growth.

Gray: Gray is typically associated with neutrality in dreams. It may suggest a lack of emotion or feeling or an impending decision on which one has yet to make up their mind.

Green: Green generally represents balance, harmony, and growth. It can symbolize renewal, fertility, or prosperity.

Orange: Orange often relates to creativity and indicates abundant energy and enthusiasm.

Pink: Pink represents love, romance, and femininity. It could also symbolize compassion and understanding.

Purple: Purple typically symbolizes mystery, spiritual awareness, or higher understanding in dreams. It can also suggest a connection to the supernatural.

Rainbow: Rainbows are often associated with hope and joy but can also signify transformation or good luck. They may represent an inner need for balance and harmony.

Red: Red can symbolize strong emotions such as love, anger, passion, and intensity. It can also represent danger or warning.

Silver: Silver typically indicates spiritual strength and inner wisdom. It can also reflect the ability to see through deception or lies.

White: White is often seen as a sign of purity and peace in dreams. It could be indicative of new beginnings and clarity of thought.

Yellow: Yellow is typically associated with joy, happiness, optimism, and good luck. It could also represent intelligence and mental clarity.

Animals

Bear: Bears represent power, authority, and leadership skills. If one appears in your dream, it could be time for you to take charge of a situation and make decisions.

Bee: Bees represent hard work, diligence, and productivity. If one appears in your dream, it may be time for you to put in more effort to reach success.

Bird: Birds represent freedom and spiritual growth. They may suggest that you take risks and make changes in your life to grow and succeed.

Butterfly: Butterflies often symbolize transformation and new beginnings. Dreaming of a butterfly could suggest you are ready to leave the past behind and embark on a new journey.

Cat: Cats often symbolize independence, grace, femininity, and mystery. They can also indicate that you are ready to explore new ideas or opportunities.

Deer: Deer typically represent grace, gentleness, and sensitivity. If one appears in your dream, it may be time for you to approach a situation with more care and understanding.

Dog: Dogs represent loyalty, protection, and devotion. Dreaming of a dog could mean it is time to put more trust in the people around you or seek help from them when needed.

Dragon: Dragons represent power, strength, and courage. Dreaming of a dragon may suggest it is time to draw upon these qualities within yourself to succeed.

Elephant: Elephants represent wisdom, strength, and patience. They may suggest you take a step back and assess your situation to move forward.

Fish: Fish in dreams often represent creativity, fertility, abundance, and luck. They could suggest that you take advantage of an opportunity presented before you.

Fox: Foxes symbolize intelligence and cunningness. Dreaming of a fox may suggest it is time to use your wit and knowledge to get ahead.

Horse: Horses represent power, strength, and endurance. They can also signify progress on your journey to reach your goals.

Lion: Lions are symbols of courage, strength, and confidence. They can also suggest that you need to be more assertive to get what you want out of life.

Monkey: Monkeys usually symbolize mischievousness and playfulness. Dreaming of a monkey may urge you to relax and have fun while pursuing your goals.

Owl: Owls are often associated with mystery, secrets, wisdom, and intuition. Dreaming of an owl may suggest that you need to trust your instincts when making decisions.

Rabbit: Rabbits usually represent fertility, abundance, and luck. They can also suggest that it is time for you to take a leap of faith to achieve success.

Rat: Rats can be seen as symbols of fear, disease, and danger. However, they can also represent adaptability and resourcefulness, allowing you to overcome obstacles.

Snake: Snakes are often seen as a symbol of transformation and spiritual growth. They can also warn you that danger or temptation is nearby, so be careful.

Tiger: Tigers represent boldness, courage, and determination. If a tiger appears in your dream, it may be time for you to draw upon these qualities within yourself to achieve success.

Wolf: Wolves are often seen as symbols of protection, guidance, and loyalty. If a wolf appears in your dream, it may mean that someone close to you will help lead you on the right path.

Numbers

One: Symbolizes unity, completion, and the beginning of something new. It can be seen as a milestone or the start of an adventure.

Two: Represents relationships, partnerships, balance, and duality. It can also refer to choices that must be made and being caught between two options.

Three: Refers to creative expression and growth. It symbolizes potential and is associated with self-expression and optimism.

Four: Associated with stability and security in life and feelings of being grounded and rooted in one's universe.

Five: Represents change and transformation, both internal (personal development) and external (environmental changes).

Six: Refers to harmony and balance. It often symbolizes the need to create a harmonious environment or situation to reach one's goals.

Seven: Associated with spiritual growth, inner wisdom, and intuition. It can also represent achievements and success.

Eight: Symbolizes abundance, prosperity, and self-confidence.

Nine: Represents life cycles, renewal, endings, beginnings, and closure of old chapters in life. It can also be a sign of new opportunities or new beginnings.

Ten: Represents completeness and wholeness that comes from achieving success after hard work and dedication. It is seen as a sign of destiny and the end of a cycle.

Eleven: Is associated with spiritual enlightenment, divine guidance, and higher awareness. It can also indicate one's spiritual path or journey.

Twelve: Symbolizes inner strength, faith in oneself and the universe, and personal power. It signifies greater insight and understanding of one's life purpose.

Thirteen: Represents intuition, prophetic dreams, visions, and the ability to see beyond the physical realm. It can also symbolize transformation and ascension.

Fourteen: Signifies good luck, success, and having everything one needs in life. It can also be seen as a reminder that help is on its way.

Fifteen: Refers to independence and freedom from past limitations or beliefs holding someone back. It signifies manifesting positive change in one's life.

Sixteen: Associated with personal growth and development, reaching new levels of understanding, wisdom, and enlightenment.

Seventeen: Represents inner strength, perseverance, and courage. It can also symbolize hope and self-empowerment.

Eighteen: Symbolizes the cycle of life and the completion of one's journey. It can signify spiritual fulfillment and enlightenment.

Nineteen: Refers to renewal, healing, and forgiveness, both on an individual level and in relationships with others. It symbolizes personal growth and transformation.

Twenty: Represents stability, balance, and security in life, along with feelings of being grounded and rooted in one's universe. It can also indicate that help is on its way.

Plants

Daffodil: The daffodil signifies new beginnings, hopes for the future, rebirth, and resurrection.

Dahlia: A dahlia represents elegance, grace, dignity, inner strength, resilience, and optimism.

Daisy: The daisy symbolizes innocence, purity, youthfulness, optimism, and joy.

Hibiscus: The hibiscus signifies beauty, femininity, love, loyalty, and peace.

Hydrangea: The hydrangea represents gratitude, appreciation, understanding, harmony, and grace.

Ivy: Ivy symbolizes loyalty, friendship, longevity, strength, resilience, and determination.

Lily: The lily signifies purity, innocence, rebirth, rejuvenation, and life after death or renewal.

Lotus: A lotus represents enlightenment, spiritual awakening, divine power, inner peace, and harmony to those who contemplate its beauty.

Marigold: A marigold symbolizes passion, courage, and strength. In many cultures, it is seen as a flower that brings good luck and joy.

Orchid: An orchid signifies love, beauty, luxury, and wealth. Its exotic beauty makes it an ideal gift to give someone you love.

Rose: A rose represents love, beauty, perfection, passion, romance, and deep emotions.

Sunflower: The sunflower symbolizes optimism, hope, and good fortune. It is a reminder that even in the darkest times, light is always at the end of the tunnel.

Tulip: The tulip signifies abundance, fertility, and prosperity. It's also believed to bring good luck in many cultures.

Body Parts

Arms: Arms signify strength, comfort, protection, and the ability to carry out tasks in your life.

Back: Backs often represent support, strength, resilience in difficult times, and a need to look back at past experiences or turn back from something to move forward with greater clarity.

Brain: The brain is associated with intellect, problem-solving, and wisdom. A dream about the brain may suggest that you need to use your analytical skills or intuition to make sense of something happening in your life.

Ears: Ears often symbolize listening and paying attention to what others say. They could also suggest that you must pay more attention to your surroundings to understand the situations around you.

Eyes: Eyes symbolize insight and seeing things clearly. Dreams about eyes may indicate a need for clarity or insight into a situation you are facing in your waking life.

Hair: Hair signifies a need for self-expression, creativity, and a desire or an urge to stand out from the crowd.

Hands: Hands represent creativity, healing, the ability to complete tasks, and the need for control or authority over something.

Head: The head symbolizes intellect, wisdom, and the need to use your mind to solve a problem or figure out a solution.

Heart: The heart is associated with emotional connections, compassion, love, understanding, and a need for emotional healing or connection in your life.

Legs/Feet: Legs and feet signify movement, progress, a journey, feeling stuck in some area of your life, and a need to move forward to achieve your goals.

Mouth: Mouths may represent expression, communication, voice, and things you need to say but cannot express due to fear or other obstacles.

Nose: The nose often symbolizes intuition, knowledge, insight, or a need for increased awareness of yourself or the world around you.

Shoulders: Shoulders are associated with support, strength, resilience when dealing with difficult situations, and a need to take responsibility and be accountable for your actions.

Skin: Skin can signify vulnerability, sensitivity, insight, and a need to protect yourself from the outside world or to be more open and accepting of others.

Stomach: The stomach can represent digestion (literally and metaphorically), security and stability, and nourishment on an emotional level.

Teeth: Teeth symbolize communication, the ability to express oneself in different situations, and a need to be more mindful of what you say or how you say it.

Conclusion

Dream deciphering is a powerful tool that can lead to deep personal insight, offering you the opportunity to explore your subconscious mind. Through dream interpretation, you can identify certain recurring patterns in your thoughts and behaviors, as well as get an understanding of your life experiences and relationships with others. Exploring the depths of your subconscious mind and understanding its hidden messages through dreams is an exciting process that can be a powerful tool for personal growth.

After reading this book on dream interpretation, you have the necessary skills to decipher different elements that may appear in your dreams and interpret their symbolism. You have a good idea of what it means to dream about places, animals, plants, colors, and body parts. Armed with a deeper level of self-awareness through dream interpreting techniques such as free association and dream journaling, you can discover more about yourself and how you experience the world around us.

In addition to uncovering vital details about one's self, it is critical to note that dreams are often an attempt by our brains to process difficult emotions or memories that have been repressed. By understanding these symbols in your dreams, you can begin to heal from past traumas or unresolved issues. It's also important to remember that dreams are not always literal interpretations of events or feelings; they may be more abstract or symbolic representations of experiences. Therefore, it's crucial for individuals seeking clarity surrounding a dream interpretation to approach them with open-mindedness and curiosity.

Finally, anyone attempting to decipher their dreams needs to treat their journey with care and respect. Although some interpretations may be uncomfortable or even painful at first, people on this spiritual journey should learn to trust their intuition and allow themselves time for reflection before making any drastic changes based on their newfound knowledge. Dream interpretation does not need to be an intimidating or overwhelming experience; rather, it should be viewed as an opportunity for growth and personal discovery through which you can reach greater levels of understanding both within yourself and concerning others around you.

Through this book, readers can finally make sense of those mysterious dreams that have been recurring in their lives. Your dreams are now accessible for further exploration, helping bring a greater understanding of yourself and where you want to go in the future. May this book help bring clarity and purpose to your life—so keep dreaming!

Part 2: Spiritual Cleansing

The Ultimate Guide to Psychic Protection, Reiki, Ways to Cleanse Your Chakras, Auras, and Raising Your Vibration

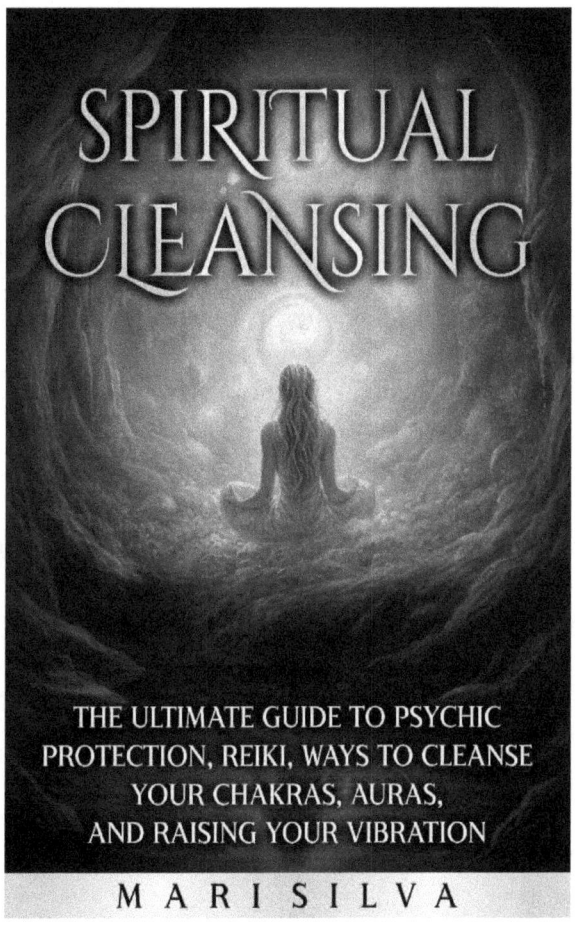

Introduction

Are you searching for ways to protect yourself from negative energy and raise your vibration? If so, you've come to the right place. In this ultimate guide to spiritual cleansing, you will learn the basics of psychic protection, how to use Reiki to send healing energy, how to cleanse and balance your chakras, clear negative energy from your aura, and raise your vibration to a higher frequency. Comprising of 10 thoroughly researched and expertly vetted chapters on all things spiritual, following the advice in this insightful book will empower you to protect yourself from negative energy and live a life of positive vibes.

Chapter one (You and Your Spiritual Welfare) will enlighten you on the significance of spiritual cleansing and welfare. It answers commonly asked questions, including:

- Why should I care about my spiritual welfare?
- Why must I learn to spiritually cleanse and protect myself or my home? What am I cleansing or protecting myself from?
- How do I know I'm cleansed and protected?
- Can anyone practice spiritual cleansing?
- And more

Through this, you will learn valuable skills to improve your quality of life and clear your mind. By examining what chakras are, where they come from, their purpose, and why they are essential, chapter two (Your Aura and Chakras 101) provides an overview of how energy flows through life forces. It gets more in-depth about each chakras symbol, their Sanskrit names, origins, location, and how they can influence you. You learn about your aura for good health, vitality, and a positive attitude.

Once you understand how your mind and body connect, chapter three (Cleansing Your Aura and Chakras) will teach you how to clear and unblock each chakra and cleanse your aura. It will get you well on the way to happiness and peace. Chapter four (Meditation to Raise Your Vibration) provides insight into vibrational frequency and how it can help you emotionally. You will discover clear, actionable, step-by-step instructions for a simple meditation exercise to raise your vibration and many more valuable tips for busy people.

Chapter 5 (The Healing Power of Reiki) introduces you to the power of Reiki, how it works, and how you can use it to your advantage. There are plenty of tips and tricks for how to put things into practice and apply them to your life. Don't worry if you're not familiar with the concept of Reiki, as the practice is thoroughly explained. Chapter six (Cleansing Energy with Reiki) gets a little more exciting with hands-on, practical exercises to clear unwanted energy through several Reiki techniques. You will learn about smudging in chapter seven (To Smudge or Not to Smudge) and why some consider this cleansing method controversial. Nonetheless, there are plenty of illustrations and clear instructions on creating your smudge stick from accessible herbs. Then, you can use smudging to cleanse yourself, the home, and other people or objects.

How is a spiritual bath different from any other bath? This question is answered in chapter eight (Spiritual Baths for Cleansing and Protection). You will discover the benefits of spiritual bathing and some creative recipes with ingredients and clear step-by-step instructions for creating a spiritual bath for cleansing and protection. In chapter nine (Crystal Purification and Protection), crystals and stones are discussed as cleansing and protection methods. A comprehensive list of various crystals you can use, and their spiritual meanings are included.

Once you've learned how to cleanse and protect yourself, you are shown how to keep others spiritually safe, wherever they are, in chapter ten (Cleansing and Protecting Your Loved Ones). The book closes with a detailed glossary of useful spiritual cleansing herbs.

Chapter 1: You and Your Spiritual Welfare

Spiritual cleansing is an integral part of maintaining your mental and emotional welfare. It is the purification of your spirit and energy field so you become more connected to your higher self and the divine essence surrounding you. Through this journey, you reconnect with your inner wisdom, gain clarity on life's challenges, and open your heart to greater joy and contentment. By engaging in metaphysical cleansing, you'll discover insight into your life's purpose and a greater sense of peace and well-being. This chapter walks you through this robust process so you can create balance and harmony within yourself and your life and release any negative energy preventing you from achieving your highest potential.

Your spiritual welfare should always be a priority.[17]

The Importance of Spiritual Welfare

Spiritual welfare is the foundation of a healthy and fulfilling life. It encompasses the well-being of the mind, body, and soul and is essential to achieve inner peace and happiness. The importance of spiritual welfare cannot be overstated, as it is crucial in shaping your thoughts, feelings, and actions.

Pursuing spiritual welfare involves developing a solid connection with your inner self and a higher power or force governing the universe. Through it, you gain direction and meaning in life and understand the reason for your existence. When spiritually fulfilled, you are better equipped to deal with the challenges and complexities of life. You are more resilient and can handle stress and adversity better. Besides that, spiritual welfare is closely linked to your physical and mental health. Research in the *Journal of Happiness Studies* shows that spiritually fulfilled people are more likely to have a positive outlook on life and are less prone to depression and anxiety. They have lower levels of stress hormones in their bodies, reducing the risk of developing chronic illnesses, such as heart disease, diabetes, and cancer. Spiritual welfare cultivates virtues like compassion, forgiveness, and gratitude. These qualities are essential to build strong and fulfilling relationships with others and create community and belonging. They encourage you to be more empathetic and understanding toward others and to see the world from different perspectives.

Ultimately, spiritual welfare is vital to lead a fulfilling and meaningful life. It enriches your life, provides a purpose, makes coping with stress and adversity easier, and promotes physical and mental well-being. You can lead a more joyful, compassionate, and productive life by prioritizing your spiritual welfare.

Spiritual Cleansing Promotes Spiritual Welfare

Spiritual cleansing is an ancient practice used for centuries to clear the mind, body, and spirit of negative energy. Its origins can be traced to various cultures and religions, including Hinduism, Buddhism, and Native American traditions.

- In Hinduism, spiritual cleansing is called *"shuddhi,"* which includes using mantras, meditation, and yoga.

- Spiritual cleansing in Buddhism is known as "purity of mind," the practice of mindfulness, meditation, and self-reflection.
- Native American traditions have unique spiritual cleansing methods, including smudging with sage, sweetgrass, or cedar.

In each method, negative energy, emotions, and thoughts are removed and replaced with positive energy.

Reasons Your Well-Being Needs a Pick-Me-Up

Spiritual pollution is an interesting concept to explore and can profoundly impact your life. It's worth taking a step back to look at contamination of the spirit and how it happens. At its core, pollution of inner health is environmental turmoil affecting spiritual well-being, and it happens in two ways.

1. Firstly, it can be caused by physical environmental factors, such as pollution, noise, and overcrowding. This toxicity can directly affect mental and emotional well-being, damaging the natural environment and disturbing your peace of mind.
2. The second way spiritual pollution can happen is through more intangible factors, like thoughts, beliefs, and values. This stress is caused by your mental and emotional state. Negative thoughts, beliefs, and values can have an insidious effect on divine connection, as they can gradually erode optimism, gratitude, and relationship with the divine.

Ultimately, spiritual pollution is something everyone needs to be mindful of. Whether physical or psychological in nature, it can devastatingly impact lives. You must be aware of your environment and thoughts and do your best to keep them free of pollution to combat it and ensure your inner health remains strong and vibrant.

How to Know if You Need Spiritual Cleansing

Everyone is exposed to a certain degree of spiritual pollution in their daily lives, through the media, environment, or even their actions. But how do you know when it's time to give your spirit a good cleansing? Here are a few signs indicating it's time to do some soul-searching and cleanse yourself of detrimental influences.

The first sign is a feeling of being stuck. If you feel stuck in a rut and unable to move forward, it may be time to look inward and clear out whatever is holding you back. It could be negative thoughts or ideas, patterns of behavior, or even toxic relationships preventing you from realizing your true potential.

Another sign is physical symptoms like fatigue, headaches, or exhaustion. If you're feeling these physical symptoms and can't shake them, it could be a sign something deeper is occurring, and possibly your spirit is weighed down by harmful energy.

The final sign is feeling disconnected from yourself and your overall purpose. If you're merely going through the motions and not living life to its fullest, it's time to take a step back and purify yourself of your ego. A spiritual cleanse can help clear negative vibrations blocking your connection to your true self and help you reconnect with your higher purpose.

With all this talk of personal wellness, you may wonder if you can use spiritual healing on non-physical things. The answer is absolute, yes. This practice is based on unfavorable energy trapped in a space, creating an atmosphere of fear, sadness, or anger if left unchecked. Purification eliminates this harmful force, creating a more positive and peaceful atmosphere in the home.

Suppose you're experiencing any of the above signs. In that case, it's time to take a step back and give yourself a good cleanse of the soul, reconnect with your true self, and move forward in life with greater clarity and purpose. The good news is anyone can engage in spiritual cleansing. It is not an activity exclusive to a particular religion or belief system. Everyone can benefit from it, regardless of their background. The key to successful metaphysical purification is focusing on yourself and your connection to the natural world.

The Role of Spiritual Cleansing and Welfare

Spiritual cleansing and welfare are concepts that have been around for centuries but have recently become more popular as people become more aware of the power of energy. It is a practice using various rituals, symbols, and techniques to clear negative energy from your life and attract positive energy.

Spiritual Energy

Spiritual energy is the vital force within and around you all the time. It is a power that exists on an energetic level, making it difficult to measure, but it is definitely there. It is the vital force connecting you to the divine world and the power to open you up to your spiritual self and the spiritual bodies of others. It is often described as a life force connected to your soul. This power helps you to become more aware of your inner self and better understand yourself and the world around you. This energy is also connected to your aura, an energetic field surrounding you.

Your aura comprises the divine power within you and helps protect you from outside influences. Energy from the spiritual realm can be used in many different ways, such as healing and manifesting. When used correctly, this divine power becomes a powerful tool to achieve your goals. It is a great way to connect to the spiritual world because it enables more awareness of the subtleties of life that are often taken for granted. By connecting to your spiritual energy, you learn to trust your intuition and use your spiritual energy to manifest what you desire in life.

How Spiritual Cleaning Affects Spiritual Energy

The role of spiritual cleansing and welfare is often misunderstood by many. But ultimately, it is the concept that each person comprises a physical body, a soul, and an aura. The physical body is what you see and feel, the soul is the energy making up your being, and the aura is the energy field surrounding you. Your physical body is as important as your spiritual state of being. Your soul comprises energies that are constantly in motion, and these energies affect physical and mental health.

- **Aura cleansing** is spiritual purification restoring the natural power of the aura, the energy field surrounding your physical body. This aura cleansing helps remove unwelcome or stagnant energy and restores the flow of vitality in the aura. It protects you from detrimental influences affecting your physical, mental, and spiritual well-being.

- **Spiritual welfare** is vital for overall well-being. It is being mindful of your soul's needs and taking steps to ensure you live in harmony with your spiritual self, including engaging in spiritual pursuits like meditation, visualization, and prayer. It is being mindful of your thoughts and feelings and ensuring you live aligned with your highest self.

When spiritually unbalanced, your energy becomes blocked or stagnant, which leads to physical, emotional, and mental issues. The ultimate goal is to foster self-awareness and spiritual growth. You become more in tune with your spiritual self and understand your spiritual needs and desires by clearing negative feelings. It helps you make choices and decisions aligned with your highest good.

Spiritual rejuvenation and welfare are important aspects of well-being. They eliminate negative energy and restore your spiritual body to its natural balance. They encourage being mindful of spiritual needs and assuring harmonious living with your true self. You can clear harmful energies, and engage in activities fostering self-awareness and spiritual growth, leading to increased well-being and balance by engaging in metaphysical exercises.

The Act of Spiritual Cleansing

Spiritual welfare is of utmost importance in today's world. Living in a world of energy, keeping your spiritual energy clean and safe is essential to ensure mental and physical well-being. Learning to detox and spiritually protect yourself or your home is essential to creating protective boundaries with people and situations that bring you down. Whether you are spiritual or not, understanding how to perform spiritual purification can be exceptionally beneficial. Listed below are a few of the many reasons for spiritual cleansing:

- To reduce stress, worry, fear, anger, doubt, or other unpleasant emotions.
- To protect yourself from external influences such as curses, hexes, or other negative energies.
- To increase your mental clarity and focus.
- To bring peace and balance into your life.
- To reduce the physical symptoms of negative energy.
- To improve relationships with others.
- To promote life purpose.
- To boost self-connection.

The main reason is that cleansing your spirit can clear bad vibrations and help you reset your energy levels. When bad energy accumulates in your life, it is hard to focus on the positive and stay in a good headspace. Performing a purifying ritual will clear away this toxic energy, allowing you to move forward with a fresh perspective. Purification will benefit you in times of stress or difficulty, as it provides calm amid the chaos to bring tranquility and peace. In addition, the act will heighten your intuition, allowing you to make better decisions and keep you in tune with your inner voice. Finally, learning to perform a spiritual cleanse connects you more deeply with the spiritual world. You learn to open up to new ideas and insights and connect to a higher power that can provide guidance and wisdom.

What Happens During and After Spiritual Cleansing?

Spiritual cleansing is a powerful process to help clear negative vibrations and reconnect with your higher self. You can open the door to manifesting desires and healing emotional trauma by setting an intention and utilizing various techniques to clear energy blocks. The action begins with an intention to clear unwanted energy blocking your spiritual progress. The best way is by visualizing a white light flowing through your body, washing away all the unwanted vibrations. Other methods include:

- Burning sage or other appropriate herbs
- Crystal healing
- Reciting mantras or affirmations
- Meditation
- Visualization
- Smudging

Once the purification is complete, you should feel lighter, more balanced, and more connected to your higher self.

What Spiritual Cleansing Looks Like

A few key elements are essential for spiritual cleansing and protection.
1. First, you need an open mind. To make the best of spiritual cleansing, you must accept that there are forces beyond what you can see or hear. It requires a willingness to take a leap of faith and be open to the possibilities existing beyond the physical world.
2. Second, you need a personal connection to the higher world through meditation, prayer, or another spiritual practice. Connecting to the spiritual realm allows you to access the energy

and healing power of the spiritual world, to purify and safeguard your life.
3. Third, you need knowledge of spiritual purification and protection techniques. There are many ways to purify and safeguard yourself, and it's important to understand the different techniques and how they work. It allows you to apply the methods to get the most out of them.
4. Finally, you must have patience and focus. The entire endeavor takes time and effort, so it's crucial to have patience and focus to stick with it because it's ultimately worth it. As you develop and refine your technique, you'll use spiritual purification and safeguarding more effectively and efficiently.

Essentially, the healing process is the only way to enhance your well-being.

What a Cleansed Spirit Feels Like

The feeling of being cleansed and protected is difficult to describe, but when you experience it, you'll know. After a good cleanse, you feel an overall sense of peace and well-being. You'll feel an increased clarity that wasn't there before and protection shielding you from the world's negative energies. It's a sensation often described as being enveloped in a bubble of peace and love. You'll experience a heightened awareness of yourself and your surroundings. As you experience this, you become more in tune with your intuition and more connected to the spiritual world. Also, you'll be less affected by the stress and negativity of the world around you and more in touch with your inner power.

Modern life can sometimes be stressful, making it easy to lose your way. Inevitably, there will be days when your cleansing feels weaker than usual, no matter how hard you work to improve yourself. However, you shouldn't worry about this, as it's easy to get back on track because everything you have done up to this point involves tuning into your inner energy, aura, and spirit. All you need to do is reconnect with yourself, usually through meditation. Meditation will clear your mind and help you connect with yourself more deeply. As you meditate, focus on being cleansed and protected. Visualize a protective bubble of light around you, and imagine the loving energy of the universe washing away the negative energy clinging to you. Ultimately, feeling rejuvenated and secure is a unique experience left to individual interpretation. This feeling cannot be forced, so take time to relax and connect with yourself, allowing the feeling to come naturally. Only then will you be closer to becoming the best version of yourself.

Spiritual cleansing is becoming increasingly popular with people of all ages and backgrounds. It's an ancient method to restore balance and harmony to the mind, body, and soul. This process is used for protection and to raise your vibration. It helps clear out stagnant chi, emotional blockages, and negative patterns in your life and is an essential part of spiritual growth and self-care. Use it to open up your spiritual energy channels, create an open and clear association with your higher self, and connect to the divine power within you. Purifying your spirit can be done through various rituals, such as using sage or palo santo to clear negative chi, using crystals or bathing to clear out unwanted energy, or meditation or chanting mantras to raise your vibration. Ultimately, spiritual cleansing is a powerful way to connect with yourself and the divine while providing protection and a higher vibration.

Chapter 2: Your Aura and Chakras 101

If you're interested in spiritual cleansing, you must know about your aura and chakras. Those who practice use their knowledge of these systems to send and receive healing energies, increase self-awareness, and manifest positive outcomes in life. This chapter explores these concepts' basics and how to manifest your highest potential. You will learn what they are, how you can sense and work with them, and the different ways to use them for personal growth. A better understanding of auras and chakras will unlock your body's potential energy to achieve your goals and fulfill your dreams. So, let's get started on your journey to unlocking your energy.

You need to gain a deeper understanding of your aura and chakras to achieve ultimate enlightenment[18]

Your Life Force

Energy has been a force flowing through every living being for centuries. It's essential for human existence, recognized as a vital component of physical and mental well-being. Many cultures have their names for this energy:

- *Qi* in Chinese medicine
- *Chi* in Japanese
- *Prana* in Ayurveda

Your energy, or qi, chi, or prana, is the force flowing throughout your body and supports your energetic existence. The chakras, the seven energy centers located throughout the body, are responsible for regulating energy flow. Each chakra is associated with a specific color, element, and body part. Each has unique properties associated with specific organs, feelings, and spiritual qualities.

The energy flowing through the chakras is often described as a river. It begins at the root chakra, at the base of the spine, and travels up through the other six chakras. Each chakra is like a dam, regulating energy circulation and ensuring it's distributed evenly throughout the body. When one chakra is blocked or not functioning correctly, it disrupts the energy flow and causes problems in other areas of the body.

Your Aura

Do you ever feel you can sense certain vibes or energy from other people? That's your aura. Your aura is the energy field surrounding the body and emanates from within. It's like a colorful halo giving insight into your emotional, physical, and spiritual state. Your aura is influenced by your chakras and vice versa. When chakras are balanced and open, your aura will be bright, vibrant, and full of positive energy. However, if your chakras are blocked or imbalanced, your aura appears dull, murky, or dark. Auras can be affected by external factors, like people and the environment.

An Overview of the Chakra System

Your aura and chakras are powerful and influential forces with the potential to shape you. They are part of the same energy system and work together, creating your overall energetic health.

- Your aura is the energy field surrounding and interpenetrating your physical body and comprises multiple energetic layers.
- Your chakras are the seven major energy centers within your aura corresponding to different physical, emotional, mental, and spiritual states of being.

How Your Aura and Chakras Connect

Your aura and chakras are closely connected and intertwined. Together, they act as a filter for the energy you take in from the outside world and the energy you expel into the world. Your aura is the energetic field surrounding your body and has distinct layers, each representing an aspect of your physical, mental, and spiritual being. These layers are connected to your seven chakras – energy centers and serve as gateways between your physical and spiritual realms. Your chakras and aura work together to keep your energy balanced and manifest your life's purpose. Your chakras' energy flows out through your aura to the external environment - the energy from the environment flows back in. When your chakras and aura are balanced, the energy flows freely, allowing positive energy, creativity, and spiritual growth. However, when your chakras and aura are out of balance, it can lead to physical, mental, and emotional blockages and negative energy. Understanding and working with your aura and chakras can increase your energy flow, balance your emotions, and create positive change in your life.

What Are Chakras?

The origin of chakras is a topic that has fascinated many people for centuries. They were developed to help people understand the complex relationship between the mind, body, and spirit. Over the years, the concept of chakras has spread beyond the borders of India. It has become a popular subject of study and practice in many parts of the world. Today, countless books, workshops, and classes are available dedicated to exploring the nature of chakras and their role in overall health and well-being.

Chakras are energy points in your body, specifically along the spine, strongly influencing your health and well-being. There are seven primary chakras:

- The Root Chakra (Muladhara)
- The Sacral Chakra (Svadhishthana)
- The Solar Plexus Chakra (Manipura)
- The Heart Chakra (Anahata)
- The Throat Chakra (Vishuddha)
- The Third Eye Chakra (Ajna)
- The Crown Chakra (Sahasrara)

Since each chakra is connected to life's physical, mental, emotional, and spiritual aspects, its vibration is associated with specific physical and spiritual attributes. They are the energy center of your body and the source of your spiritual power. You and your chakras are intrinsically linked. Each of the seven chakras is connected to a specific part of the body, a specific emotion, and the energies flowing through them. For example:

- The root chakra is related to the physical body.
- The heart chakra is related to the emotional body.
- The crown chakra is related to the spiritual body.

All your chakras are connected, forming a single, unified energy field; this is your aura. Your aura is more than just a colorful, ethereal energy field surrounding you. It's the sum of energy emitted by all your chakras combined. The chakras are the energy centers in your body that take in and transmit energy, from physical to emotional and then to spiritual. Each chakra has a specific purpose, and when you're out of balance, it is reflected in your aura. If one of your chakras is blocked, unbalanced, or overactive, it causes your aura to become stagnant or murky, leading to physical, mental, emotional, and spiritual issues.

On the other hand, when all your chakras are balanced, your aura radiates bright, vibrant energy. You can see from this that your chakras are directly related to your aura. If you want to maintain a healthy aura, you must take care of your chakras so that they can take in and transmit energy appropriately.

Why You Need to Learn about Your Chakras

Chakras are essential for spiritual awareness and development. Practitioners believe that by understanding and working with chakras, you can restore balance, heal, and reach higher states of consciousness.

All life force flows from the sacral chakra to the crown chakra, which simultaneously demands all seven to be open. When this happens, they align with the universe, providing greater insight and clarity. By understanding the chakras and their interaction, you'll better understand how your body and mind work together. With this knowledge, you become more aware of your inner self and feelings, more mindful of your physical and mental health, better decision-making, and live as your true self. In addition to physical and psychological health, the chakras help you become more spiritually conscious. You'll grow more in tune with your spiritual self as you work with them.

If you feel something is off or want to take the next step in your spiritual journey, you know where to look. Connecting with your chakras can open up a whole new world of possibilities and help you tap into the power within.

The Seven Chakras

The following comprehensive guide offers an in-depth exploration of the chakras, unveiling their hidden secrets and providing a clear road map to achieving and maintaining balance. Learn the scientific basis behind the chakras, their associated elements, and the spiritual significance of their location in the body.

The Root Chakra (Muladhara)

The root chakra, or *Muladhara*, is the first energy center in the chakra system. It is a Sanskrit word meaning "root support" or "foundation." This chakra is located at the base of the spine, associated with red, and is the foundation of your energetic system. The root chakra is the energy center that essentially grounds you in your physical body and the physical world. Associated with the earth element, it is the source of your basic survival

The root chakra.[19]

needs, responsible for your physical security, safety, and survival instincts. It's related to your sense of stability and foundation. You access your inner strength, courage, and determination from this energy center. The root chakra is the energy center of your physical body, which is why it is so important. When balanced and healthy, you feel safe, secure, and grounded in your physical form. As the foundation of your energetic system and the source of your inner strength and courage, it helps you access your inner power, strength, creativity, and passion. You might feel anxious, fearful, and overwhelmed when it is out of balance.

When your root chakra is open, you have access to the source of the physical world and your basic survival needs.

To open your root chakra, practitioners use meditation, yoga, and self-awareness. Additionally, thinking positively and practicing gratitude are helpful. A diet rich in vitamins, minerals, and proteins helps restore balance. Other methods like sound therapy and aromatherapy can open the root chakra.

The Sacral Chakra (Svadhishthana)

The sacral chakra, or *Svadhishthana*, is located 2-3 inches below the navel at the lower end of the spine. This chakra is associated with orange and is the source of your creative and sexual energy. "Svadhishthana" is derived from the Sanskrit words "*svadhi*" (meaning "self") and "*sthana*" (meaning "place"). It is the center of your emotional being, governing your feelings, desires, and relationships. When this chakra is open, you experience the full range of feelings without fear. The

Sacral chakra.[20]

sacral chakra is associated with the water element, more closely linked to your bodily fluids, and responsible for the energy flow between your physical body and your spiritual being.

Connected with pleasure and creativity, it is responsible for your desire and ability to experience healthy connections and intimacy. When the sacral chakra is open and balanced, you can fully express your feelings and desires and are free to explore and enjoy your sexuality. When the sacral chakra is blocked or out of balance, you experience various physical and psychological symptoms, including lower back pain, lethargy, lack of motivation, and difficulty expressing emotions and desires. Practitioners have reported feeling disconnected from their spiritual side and experiencing guilt, shame, or fear of their sexuality.

The sacral chakra is one of the most integral energy centers in the human body and is an integral part of your overall well-being. Engaging in activities allowing you to express your emotions and desires and fully enjoy your sexuality ensures this chakra is open and balanced. Activities include yoga, meditation, and creative pursuits like art and music. Practicing self-care is equally important, as you will nurture and connect with your spiritual side.

The Solar Plexus Chakra (Manipura)

The solar plexus chakra, or *Manipura*, is an energy center in the abdominal region. This chakra is responsible for your personal power and is associated with yellow. The name Manipura is derived from Sanskrit, meaning "lustrous gem." The solar plexus chakra is located below your ribs, near the navel, where the three major energy channels, *ida*, *pingala*, and *sushumna*, meet. It is related to the digestive system and the endocrine glands, specifically the pancreas, adrenals, and liver.

Solar plexus chakra.[21]

This chakra is associated with the element of fire and is the center of energy and dynamism. When the solar plexus chakra is balanced, you feel strong and self-confident. You can take the initiative and make decisions, be creative and brave, and have a strong sense of self-worth. Your purpose in life becomes clear, or you feel less stressed because of your good sense of direction.

When the solar plexus chakra is out of balance, you experience insecurity, fear, and low self-esteem. Powerlessness and lack of control overcome you, and some practitioners noted experiencing physical manifestations such as digestive problems, fatigue, and diabetes. Practice yoga and meditation, and focus on your breath to bring the solar plexus chakra back into balance. You can practice visualization and affirmations and focus on activities bringing joy and happiness. Crystals and gemstones like citrine, yellow jade, and amber help bring this chakra back into balance. Finally, surround yourself with yellow to help remind you of your personal power.

The Heart Chakra (Anahata)

The heart chakra, or *Anahata*, is in the center of the chest and has a deep spiritual meaning and significance. The meaning of the word Anahata is "unhurt" or "unstuck," referring to the fact that this chakra is the center of love, compassion, and connection. The color associated with the heart chakra is green, symbolizing growth, harmony, and balance. The origin of the heart chakra comes from the subtleties of the body, the energy field related to all emotions and feelings. Its location is in the chest, just behind the sternum, at the same level as the heart. The heart chakra is associated with love, kindness, compassion, and acceptance and is the center of the higher self. It bridges the physical and spiritual realms and the connection between the conscious and subconscious minds.

Heart chakra.[22]

When the heart chakra is open and balanced, you experience peace and harmony and become more open to receiving and giving love. The heart chakra is associated with trust, faith, and the ability to forgive. It is the gateway to higher consciousness and facilitates the connection to your divine nature. When it is open, you cultivate a deep connection to the divine and experience unconditional love in your life.

When the heart chakra is out of balance, you feel disconnected from your spiritual self and unable to feel joy and love. Practitioners observed the symptoms of an imbalanced heart chakra, including depression, anxiety, and disconnection from others. Meditation, yoga, and other mindfulness practices have proved useful in bringing balance to the heart chakra. Using crystals and essential oils helps open and balance the heart chakra.

Ultimately, the heart chakra is essential to your spiritual journey and supports self-awareness, love, kindness, and compassion for yourself and others. By balancing the heart chakra, you experience a deep spiritual connection and open yourself to experience unconditional love.

The Throat Chakra (Vishuddha)

The throat chakra, or *Vishuddha*, is located in the throat area. This chakra is associated with the element of Ether, and its color is blue. Vishuddha means "purification," reflecting its purpose in the body. The throat chakra is the fifth chakra and the bridge between the heart and the mind. It is the center of communication, expression, and creativity. When this chakra is blocked, it leads to insecurity, difficulty communicating, and a lack of creativity. The throat chakra is associated with the thyroid gland, the lungs, the vocal cords, the neck, and the jaw. When this chakra is balanced, it regulates metabolism and improves the functioning of the lungs. It encourages the healthy operation of the immune system and increases communication and creativity. The throat chakra is associated with true emotion. It promotes honesty and authenticity when balanced. To better understand your feelings, this chakra opens up the gateway to self-expression.

Throat chakra.[23]

Practitioners noted that this chakra fosters purpose and a greater connection to the divine when fully opened. It helps improve relationships and generates inner peace and harmony.

Third eye chakra.[24]

The Third Eye Chakra (Ajna)

The third eye chakra, or *Ajna*, is the sixth primary energy center of the body. It is located between the eyebrows, just above the bridge of the nose, and is represented by the color indigo. This chakra is associated with psychic ability and is often called the "*mind's eye.*" The origin of the third eye chakra dates back to ancient India, where it was believed to be the seat of wisdom and intuition. In yoga, the third eye chakra is the first to open, allowing access to the higher realms of consciousness. As the third eye chakra is activated, it develops intuition and the ability to perceive the spiritual realm. The third eye chakra is associated with the element of light, developed through meditation. Working with this chakra helps to open your mind, allowing you to tap into your inner wisdom. It is associated with the pineal gland, which regulates the hormones governing your feelings, sleep, and stress.

When the third eye chakra is balanced, it reduces fear and anxiety and increases peace and contentment. It is associated with the pine cone, symbolizing the gateway to the higher realms of consciousness. When it is open and balanced, you have more access to your inner wisdom and insight into the deeper mysteries of life.

The Crown Chakra (Sahasrara)

The crown chakra, or *Sahasrara*, is the highest of the chakras and the most divine. It is the source of spiritual energy and is the primary center for enlightenment and divine wisdom. The crown chakra is associated with violet and white and is located at the top of the head. The origin of Sahasrara comes from the ancient Hindu practice of Kundalini yoga. The crown chakra is activated during this practice, opening the gateway to spiritual consciousness and divine connection. It is often called the "thousand-petaled lotus" or "thousand-spoked wheel." The crown chakra is about connecting with the divine and transcending the physical realm. It is associated with spiritual awakening, enlightenment, self-realization, and ultimate spiritual transformation. When open, practitioners report a higher consciousness and are the source of divine wisdom, cosmic knowledge, and consciousness.

Crown chakra.[25]

The human body is complex and fascinating. You can go beyond the physical form and explore the energy radiating around you. That energy is your aura and is affected by your thoughts, emotions, and other influences. You can strengthen and balance your aura through the chakras. Chakras are energy centers correlating to different areas of the body. You can experience physical, mental, and emotional symptoms when they are out of balance. By working with your chakras, you can balance and harmonize your energy and create a stronger, healthier aura. Essentially, your aura and chakras are an integral part of your being, and taking the time to nurture and nourish them creates a strong and vibrant energy field.

Chapter 3: Cleansing Your Aura and Chakras

Cleansing your aura and chakras is an essential practice for keeping your energy level high and your mind clear. This spiritual tradition offers a way to balance your body, mind, and spirit. It involves cleansing your energy field of obstructions, negativity, or stagnant energy and restoring it to its natural, vibrant state. You achieve a greater sense of balance, clarity, and peace through meditation, visualization, and other techniques. This chapter explores how you can increase your energy, improve your mental and emotional well-being, and manifest your desires more easily through regular cleansing of your aura and chakras. Whether seeking to deepen your spiritual practice or wanting to stay centered in a chaotic world, cleansing your aura and chakras is a great way to start.

Meditation and visualization will help you reach a higher state of mind.[26]

Cleansing Your Seven Chakras

Your aura is the energy center of your body, and it must be cleansed regularly to avoid blockage in the energy flow. Regular cleansing of your chakras helps remove negative energy and stress from your body, leaving your aura full of positivity and joy. It improves your mental and physical health and eliminates the impurities from your energy field, making it more vibrant and powerful. Cleansing your aura and chakras will build self-confidence and self-awareness as it clarifies your thoughts and feelings. Moreover, it balances your feelings, helping you to stay focused and connected with your inner being. The following methods for each chakra will keep your energy balanced and in harmony with the universe.

The Root Chakra (Muladhara)

Have you ever felt stuck in a rut? Like, no matter what you do, you can't seem to move forward? It could signify that your root chakra is blocked. This chakra is the foundation of your energy system and governs your sense of security and stability. When blocked, it feels like the ground has been pulled out from under you. You feel disconnected from your sense of belonging, safety, and sometimes your body. It leads to anxiety, fear, panic, and depression. Physically, you may experience lower back pain, digestive issues, and a general imbalance. Unblocking your root chakra is a major step toward balance and harmony in your life. You will feel:

- A newfound confidence and stability
- More grounded, centered in your body, and less easily swayed by external forces
- More connected to your physical environment, with a deeper appreciation for the natural world's beauty and abundance
- Improved digestion, elimination, and overall vitality
- More energized and less prone to fatigue
- Chronic health issues resolve themselves

Fortunately, various techniques are available to cleanse and unblock your root chakra. The first step is to know the source of the blockages and practice mindfulness to understand where your energy is blocked. Visualization is a powerful tool. Imagine a red light radiating from the base of your spine. Visualize this energy moving up and out of your body. Feel the energy vibrating and activating all the cells in your body.

Other techniques include:
- Using affirmations. Repeat positive statements such as, "I am safe and secure" and "I am connected to my source of power."
- Practice yoga postures specifically designed to open the root chakra, such as child's pose and mountain pose.
- Spend time in nature, as being in the presence of the elements helps connect you to the Earth's energy.
- Listening to calming music, meditating, and spending time with loved ones are beneficial.

The Sacral Chakra (Svadhishthana)

The sacral chakra is responsible for your creativity, feelings, and sexuality. When this chakra is blocked, it can lead to disconnection from the physical and emotional realms. It manifests in numerous ways, from feeling emotionally blocked and unable to express yourself to feeling stuck in an unfulfilling job or relationship. When you have a blocked sacral chakra, you feel like you're being held back, with no outlet for your creative energy and passions. You may experience fear of change, low self-esteem, and shame and guilt. Physically, you may feel lethargic, drained of energy, and have difficulty focusing. You may even experience physical symptoms such as digestive issues and a lack of sexual desire. How does it feel when you unblock this powerful energy center? You'll notice:

- Inspiration flows effortlessly through you
- Ideas and solutions to problems that were once insurmountable suddenly become clear and accessible
- A heightened pleasure and sensuality
- A greater appreciation for the world's beauty around you
- A newfound ability to fully enjoy life's simple pleasures

But, perhaps the most profound effect of unblocking your sacral chakra is deep emotional healing. Old wounds and traumas buried for years can finally surface, allowing you to confront and process them healthily. It leads to greater self-awareness and a more authentic connection to your true self.

You can use various techniques to cleanse and unblock your sacral chakra and restore your balance. Firstly, you can use meditation to access the energy of your sacral chakra.

1. Sit comfortably, close your eyes, and focus on your breath. Imagine a bright orange light entering your body just below the navel. Spend a few minutes visualizing the light entering and surrounding your sacral chakra. This will open and activate your sacral chakra's energy, allowing it to flow freely.
2. Use crystals, specifically orange stones like carnelian, coral, and orange calcite. Place the stone on your lower abdomen and lie down for a few minutes. Visualize the crystal's energy entering your sacral chakra, unlocking it, and restoring balance.
3. Practice yoga asanas, like the Half-Bound Lotus pose and Hip Openers.
4. Eat a healthy and balanced diet. Eating foods rich in vitamins and minerals, like fruit, vegetables, and nuts, will nourish your body and help restore your aura.

The Solar Plexus Chakra (Manipura)

When your solar plexus is blocked, it can be uncomfortable. This chakra is located between the navel and the diaphragm and is the third chakra of the body. When it is blocked, you feel a lack of direction or power or feel stuck. You feel anxious, overwhelmed, and powerless, as if you cannot take control of your life. You experience physical symptoms such as indigestion, headaches, or fatigue. You experience low self-esteem and insecurity. When the solar plexus chakra is blocked, it can be difficult to move forward in life. You may be unable to break free because you constantly struggle with self-doubt and lack of confidence, making deciding or taking action difficult. But when you unblock your solar plexus chakra, it's like a burst of sunshine in your life.

- You feel empowered, confident, and ready to take on the world
- You no longer second-guess yourself or doubt your abilities
- You trust your intuition and have a clear purpose
- Physically, you notice increased energy and better digestion
- Emotionally, you are more in control of your thoughts and feelings
- You no longer let external factors dictate your mood or outlook on life
- You have inner peace and contentment

Affirmations are one of the most effective ways to unblock your solar plexus chakra. Positive affirmations increase your self-confidence and encourage you to take action to achieve your goals.

Other techniques include:

- Practicing mindful meditation. It focuses your attention on the present moment and emotional state to bring you clarity and reduce stress and anxiety.
- Breathwork. Take time to sit in a comfortable position and take slow, deep breaths. It raises awareness of the solar plexus chakra area in the diaphragm. You will become more relaxed and aware of your physical and emotional state.
- Practicing yoga. Many yoga poses, such as the Boat Pose, the Sun Salutation, and the Warrior I, can open this chakra.

The Heart Chakra (Anahata)

When your heart chakra is blocked, it can lead to a wide range of physical, emotional, and spiritual issues. Physically, a blocked heart chakra can manifest as chest pain, difficulty breathing, poor circulation, and heart palpitations. Emotionally, it can lead to loneliness, isolation, lack of empathy and joy, and depression. Spiritually, it can lead to a feeling of disconnection from the world, not feeling part of something larger than yourself, and a lack of purpose.

What does it feel like when your heart chakra is blocked? Generally, it feels like your heart is being squeezed – like you're disconnected from your emotions, don't have the energy to reach out to others, and are stuck in despair. It makes it difficult to experience joy, contentment, and connection to the world around you. Fortunately, you can use various techniques to cleanse your heart chakra and balance your life.

- **Practice self-love.** You need to recognize and appreciate your self-worth to unblock your heart chakra. Spend time with yourself, practice self-care, and remind yourself of your positive qualities. It will help you open up to love and connection with others.
- **Practice yoga and meditation.** These activities have the power to open and balance your energy centers, including the heart chakra. Focusing on your breath, repeating mantras, and practicing yoga postures clarifies and balances your life.

- **Surround yourself with positive energy.** Spend time with friends and family who make you feel uplifted and connected. Distance yourself from negative people and situations, and make time to relax and nurture your spirit.
- **Permit yourself to feel.** Recognize and accept your feelings, no matter how uncomfortable they are. Allow yourself to express how you feel, and don't be afraid to speak the truth, even to yourself.

The Throat Chakra (Vishuddha)

When your throat chakra is blocked, it can be a difficult and uncomfortable experience. The throat chakra is associated with communication and self-expression, so it's hard to find the words to express yourself when it is blocked. A blocked throat chakra is described as a lump in the throat or tightness in the chest as if something is stopping you from speaking. You may feel you cannot truly express yourself or are being silenced. You could experience physical symptoms such as a sore throat, hoarseness, difficulty swallowing, and neck and shoulder tension. Emotionally, you could feel frustrated, fearful, and anxious and have difficulty speaking up for yourself or expressing your needs. All these feelings and physical symptoms are signs that your throat chakra is blocked and needs attention. But what happens when you finally free it? It feels like a breath of fresh air.

- You feel a release as if a weight has been lifted off your shoulders.
- Expressing yourself authentically, without fear of judgment or rejection, is easier.
- Words flow effortlessly, so you become more confident in communicating effectively.
- Physically, you feel lightness in your throat area, as if the tension has been released.
- You notice an improvement in your overall health, as the throat chakra is connected to the thyroid gland and immune system.

There are various techniques for cleansing your throat chakra.

- One of the most popular methods is to practice chanting "OM," a vibration to cleanse and open the throat chakra. Chants like mantras "OM Shanti OM" or "OM Namah Shivaya" also work

wonders for opening the energy channels in the throat.
- Another technique is to practice yoga asanas specifically targeting the throat chakra, including poses like the Shoulder stand, Plow, Fish, and Cobra. These poses help open up the throat's energy and allow better communication.
- You can practice visualization to free your throat chakra. Visualize a blue light radiating from your throat and connecting you with the divine. As the light shines brighter, feel the tension in the area melt away.
- Finally, practice deep breathing. It relaxes the throat muscles and encourages the energy to flow freely. Take deep, calming breaths and focus on the energy in your throat.

The Third Eye Chakra (Ajna)

When your third eye chakra is blocked, it feels like you are living life on autopilot and lacking purpose. When things get rough, you become aware you're stuck in the same patterns, unable to break free. When you can't see the bigger picture, you blame yourself because you cannot trust your intuition which helps you to see it clearly. You may find it hard to focus and concentrate and have difficulty making decisions or finding clarity. Interpreting and understanding your feelings and those of others is difficult. You feel disconnected from your intuition and spiritual guidance. You may struggle with restlessness and anxiety, depression, confusion, and a lack of inspiration. These are signs that your third eye chakra is blocked. But when you free your third eye chakra, the real magic happens in your perception. Suddenly, you see things differently.

- Colors appear brighter
- Shapes are more defined
- You experience heightened intuition, as if you can sense things beyond the physical realm

It's not uncommon to feel a sense of awe and wonder at this newfound perception as you connect to something greater than yourself. It's a truly profound experience that can change how you see the world.

The good news? There are various techniques for cleansing and unblocking it to connect more with your higher self.

- One of the most common ways to free your third eye chakra is through meditation. Focusing your attention on your third eye

and repeating affirmations like "I trust my intuition" can break through blocks and open your third eye chakra.
- Visualization is another great way to cleanse and unblock this chakra. Visualize a white light coming in and opening your third eye, allowing your intuition to flow freely.
- Crystals, specifically amethyst, sodalite, and lapis lazuli, create alignment and balance by interacting with the body's aura. Place the crystal over your third eye or hold it while meditating to free it.
- Yoga is an excellent method. Poses like the Bridge and the Plow enhance the body's energy flow. As you move through these poses, focus on your third eye and visualize it opening.
- Finally, using essential oils like lavender and jasmine aromatherapy will open and balance your third eye chakra. You can diffuse the oils in your home or use them in an aromatherapy massage.

The Crown Chakra (Sahasrara)

When your crown chakra, the highest of the seven chakras, is blocked, it can create a disconnection from yourself and the world around you. You might feel stuck in a state of anxiety, depression, or confusion. It manifests in physical symptoms, such as headaches, fatigue, and poor concentration. It can lead to spiritual issues, like a lack of motivation or an inability to focus on spiritual matters - perhaps you're constantly questioning your life's purpose and feel disconnected from your true self. It can be a difficult and disorienting experience, like living in a fog and being unable to connect with the real you. You may feel trapped in your mind and unable to move forward with your life. If your crown chakra is blocked, you must take steps to free it to experience joy, peace, and connection. Unblocking your crown chakra is a life-changing experience. It's like removing a veil covering your eyes, preventing you from seeing life's beauty and magic.

- You're more connected to your higher self
- Intuition is easier to access
- You're more aware of the synchronicities and signs the universe is sending you
- You feel more grounded and centered

- You can navigate life better

Luckily, there are various techniques for cleansing your crown chakra and restoring balance to your life.

- One of the best ways is through meditation. By sitting quietly and focusing on your breath, you can tap into the energy of this chakra, refocus and restore balance. During your meditation, imagine a white or golden light radiating from the top of your head.
- Certain yoga poses can open the crown chakra and balance the body and mind. Use poses like the Lotus, Padmasana, Corpse Pose, or Savasana for peace and harmony.
- Aromatherapy using essential oils like jasmine, frankincense, and rose can create calmness and serenity. Add a few drops of your chosen oil to a diffuser and breathe in the aroma throughout the day.
- Clear quartz, amethyst, and selenite are all excellent crystals for this chakra. Place one or more of these crystals on the crown of your head while you meditate or rest.

As an extra tip, eat foods associated with each color and element of the chakra you want to free to help you cleanse and balance your chakras. For example, root vegetables like carrots and beets can help with the root chakra, while fruit like oranges and pineapples can help with the sacral chakra.

How to Meditate and Visualize

Meditation and visualization are the two most popular techniques for unblocking your chakras. Here are some tips for these methods.

Basic Meditation

To begin your meditation practice, find a comfortable place where you can sit or lie down, preferably with no distractions. Close your eyes and focus on your breathing. Take deep breaths, inhaling through your nostrils and exhaling slowly. Allow your thoughts to come and go without judgment. Keep your mind in the present moment and be conscious of your thoughts without reacting. Visualize yourself in a state of peace and tranquility and let go of negative or anxious thoughts.

Focus on each chakra, one at a time. Visualize each chakra's color, element, purpose, and location as you focus on the sensations you experience. Meditation can be done for as little as five minutes a day or as long as you like. As you practice more often, it will be easier to reach a state of complete meditation and reap the benefits.

Basic Visualization

Visualization is a powerful technique for freeing chakras and allowing energy to flow freely. To begin visualizing, find a comfortable spot and settle. Take a few deep breaths, inhaling and exhaling slowly. As you breathe, focus on the area that needs healing and envision a bright, golden light entering this area and filling it with warmth and healing energy. Visualize the chakras opening up, allowing the prana to flow. For example, picture the energy flowing through the body like a river, or envision different colors radiating from the chakras. Visualization is a powerful tool for freeing chakras, and with practice and patience, it can profoundly change your energy field.

Aura and chakras are your body's energy centers and must be cleansed regularly to avoid obstructions in the energy flow. If you've felt a shift in the room without an explanation or had a negative thought creep up and linger in your mind for days, your aura and chakras could need cleansing. Cleansing is an ancient practice used for thousands of years by practitioners to feel more grounded, balanced, and connected to the universe. It is a simple yet powerful technique to restore your natural energy and amplify your spiritual well-being.

Regular cleansing focuses on the area of each chakra with a specific technique. Cleansing opens the door to clarity, creativity, and higher consciousness when done correctly. Cleansing your chakras is an essential part of spiritual practice and a powerful tool for improving overall health and well-being.

Chapter 4: Meditation to Raise Your Vibration

Meditation is a powerful tool to help you raise your vibration, create positive energy, and find inner peace. When your vibration is raised to a higher frequency, it naturally attracts more positive experiences. Your thoughts' vibrations impact how you experience life in many ways. With meditation, you can learn to control and raise your thoughts and intentions' vibrations to manifest positive results in all areas of life with meditation.

Vibrational frequency plays a pivotal role in your journey to enlightenment.[97]

This chapter explores the concept of vibrational frequency and how it relates to meditation. It discusses the basics of this simple yet profound practice. It provides a step-by-step guide to meditating to raise your vibration and explains how to make the most of this experience, including tips on modifying the meditation for busy readers who may not always have the time or patience for a long session.

What Is Vibrational Frequency: How Can It Help

Vibrational frequency is the concept of energy flowing through and around the body at all times. All living things emit a particular vibration, either positive or negative.

Low vibrational frequencies are associated with negative emotions like sadness, anger, and fear. The more negative thoughts and emotions experienced, the lower the vibration. On the other hand, high vibrational frequencies are associated with positive emotions like joy, love, and gratitude. The vibrations rise when you open your heart and mind to love and positivity.

Raising your vibration increases your energy and frequency to attract more positive experiences. It is achieved by changing your thoughts and feelings about yourself and the world around you. Transformation happens when your thoughts shift from negative to positive, creating a higher vibrational state.

The Benefits of Raising Your Vibration

One of the most powerful practices is raising your vibration when improving your overall well-being and finding true fulfillment. You can transform many aspects of your life by boosting your energetic frequency. Here are some of the most profound benefits you can experience when raising your vibration:

Improved Mental and Emotional Well-being

You can experience heightened mental and emotional well-being by raising your vibrational frequency. As your vibration rises, the negative energy you have been carrying dissipates and is replaced with peace and contentment. Staying grounded in positive thoughts and emotions is much easier, and you will become less prone to depression or anxiety.

Clarity and Focus

When the vibration is raised, you can access higher awareness and understanding. You become more in tune with yourself, the world around you, and how you fit into it. Many people struggle with scattered thoughts or are overwhelmed, but when you raise your energetic frequency, you develop a sharper mental focus and better understand the path ahead. This heightened consciousness can lead to greater self-awareness and clarity.

Healthier Connections

The higher the vibrational frequency, the healthier and more meaningful your connections with others become. When you increase your energetic vibration, it's much easier to attract like-minded people on the same level as you are emotionally and spiritually. Your friends and family can help you to stay on track manifesting the life of your dreams.

You can give and receive love more freely, creating a solid foundation to express yourself honestly. With each connection you make, your confidence will grow as you find joy in being part of something greater than yourself.

Increased Abundance

The more you raise your vibration, the more abundance you can experience. It's like a ripple effect - the higher your vibration, the more space you create for increased quantity to enter. Abundance comes in many forms; financial resources, opportunities, relationships, and health.

Changing your mindset and focusing on what you want instead of what you don't have opens up more possibilities and attracts abundance.

The Effects of Low Vibration

Low vibration energies can have the opposite effect. This energy is associated with negativity, stagnation, and unhappiness. It hinders the ability to create positive experiences for you and those around you. The lower the vibrational frequency, the less likely it is that you will attract what you want.

Low-vibration feelings can lead to unhealthy life patterns. You may get stuck in cycles of negative thinking, and it becomes harder to break free from them. Without raising your vibration to a higher frequency, you will more likely experience fear, anger, or helplessness and be consumed by these emotions.

Although low-vibration energy seems overwhelming, there are ways to raise your vibration and experience its positive effects. You can learn how to shift your frequency and become a powerful manifesto of all good things with practice.

How Meditating and Raising Your Vibration Can Change Your Life

The best way to raise your vibration is through meditation. Through regular meditation practice, you increase the energy frequency and become more consciously aware of thoughts and feelings. This heightened awareness helps develop authentic connections, and meditation allows you to become more open and accepting of life's changes. Here is a simple yet effective meditation exercise to raise your vibration:

1. Start by Grounding Yourself

Grounding yourself is an essential first step in meditation practice. Grounding helps reduce stress and anxiety and also helps you to feel more connected to your body and the physical world around you. By grounding yourself, you can better tap into the energy of your higher vibrations and focus on what matters most.

Sit or lie on the floor and consciously connect with your breath. Take deep breaths and focus on feeling safely grounded and connected to the Earth, like being rooted like a tree or standing firmly on solid ground. This will help you feel more present and related to the energy around you. Take a few moments to feel grounded before moving on to the next step.

2. Practice Breathing Exercises to Raise Your Vibration

Inhale deeply through your nose and exhale slowly through your mouth. As you breathe in, imagine the energy from the universe entering and filling all your cells with light. As you exhale, visualize negative energy leaving your body and returning to its source. Repeat this breathwork for several minutes, focusing on your breath and feeling filled with light energy.

3. Posing Techniques to Increase Your Frequency

Next, take a few moments to move into various poses to help raise your vibration even further. Stand comfortably with your feet firmly planted on the ground. Take a few deep breaths, focus on opening your heart, and let go of negative or blocked energy. Then, slowly raise your arms above your head in a V-shape and take another deep breath, imagining all the universe's frequencies entering your fingertips as you reach the sky. Continue to explore various poses to open up your body, release negativity, and allow the energies around you to fill you.

4. Incorporate Visualization Techniques to Stay Centered

While in these poses, imagine yourself surrounded by an orb of white light for a few moments. This light is filled with healing energy and protection from negative frequencies. Imagine being energized by this light and feeling more connected to your highest self. Visualize radiating with light and energy and feeling more open, expansive, and connected; let the light fill you and cleanse your energy.

Meditating on the Go: Tips for Busy People

Meditation can be a challenging activity to maintain, especially when you lead a hectic lifestyle. Fortunately, with a few creative strategies, it is possible to cultivate and embody mindfulness even in your busiest moments.

Set Aside 10 Minutes a Day

Dedicate 10-15 minutes of your day to meditation. Even if it's only 10 minutes, it can help you to stay focused and connected to yourself and the energies around you. You don't need much time for meditation; even a few minutes can make a difference in your day.

When you start, don't put too much pressure on yourself. Start small and increase the time when it feels comfortable to do so. Set your phone's alarm to remind you to take 10 minutes for a mini meditation session.

Use Guided Meditations

If you don't have the time or energy to sit down and practice traditional meditation, try guided meditation. Plenty of free and paid audio recordings can help you to relax and re-center yourself. Start with a simple breathing exercise and gradually move on to different guided meditations as you become more comfortable.

Look for an app to help make meditation more accessible, like those designed specifically for people with busy lives. You can use these apps to guide and remind you when and where to practice mindfulness for a short period, whether for 5 minutes or an hour.

Take Advantage of Small Pockets of Time

Taking short breaks throughout the day gives you time to reset your mind and re-energize your body. These moments are essential for cultivating mindfulness but don't require dedicated chunks of time exclusively for meditation practice.

While waiting in line, on public transportation, or taking a lunch break, become aware of your breath and observe sensations arising within your body without judgment or attachment.

Practice Mindful Breathing

If you can't get away from work during the day, practice mindful breathing wherever you are, at your desk, or walking down the street if necessary. All it takes is five minutes to focus on your breath movement and relax into stillness before returning to your task.

Allow yourself this small gesture of compassion. Permit yourself to step out and practice self-reflection whenever needed. It could be as simple as taking one deep breath before beginning a difficult task or project during work hours.

Get Creative with Your Practice

There are many ways to incorporate meditation without sitting still for long periods. Walking or running is a form of moving meditation. Focus on the present moment and be mindful during your daily tasks. For example, folding laundry can become a mindful task if you pay attention to the feeling of the fabric in your hands and focus on each article as you fold it.

Use Your Morning and Evening Commutes

Your morning commute might not seem like the ideal place for meditation, but with the right attitude, it can be done. If traveling by public transport, use this time instead of checking emails or scrolling through social media. Harness this period by training your attention on something more productive, like conscious breathing while staring out the window.

Listen to relaxing music to help clear your mind clutter and tune inwards rather than being distracted by what's happening around you. Prepare mentally for what lies ahead at work or home after returning from the commute.

Bring Meditation Practices into Your Everyday Activities

Meditation can be something other than a dedicated practice. You can bring mindfulness into your everyday activities, such as washing dishes, gardening, or taking a shower, by focusing on the present moment and being aware of what is happening around you. It helps with relaxation and creating peace within yourself.

You can practice mindful eating, an exceptionally great habit to form when trying to stay focused on healthy habits. Before eating, take a moment to notice the food in front of you - its color, aroma, texture, etc. You will appreciate the food and savor every bite rather than mindlessly snacking.

Incorporate Walking Meditations into Your Daily Routine

Walking meditations are a great way to become more aware and present in your body. They can be done indoors or outdoors and focus on each step and sensations arising in the body during the process.

Start by taking slow and deliberate steps with mindful awareness of each footfall. As you walk, note the surrounding scenery and sounds and allow your senses to be fully engaged. You can add breathing exercises into the routine by focusing on the breath's rhythm as you walk.

Stay Consistent

Consistency is the key to making a practice a regular part of your life. Set a reminder every day to take time out for yourself and meditate. The more consistent you are with your practice, the easier it will become.

Remember, meditation is not about achieving perfection but connecting to yourself in the moment. The more you practice, the more mindful moments you can incorporate into your everyday life.

More Ways to Raise Your Vibration

The practice of meditation is an essential tool to raise your vibration to become more present and connected. There are many ways to raise your vibration.

Get Out in Nature: Nature has unique ways of lifting your spirits and raising your vibration. Taking the time to get out in nature, whether a simple walk in the park or an extended hike in the mountains, can be incredibly therapeutic for the body and mind. When you are outside, surrounded by trees, animals, plants, and fresh air, you reconnect with yourself and recharge your energy.

Plan Small Vacations: Nothing can raise your vibration like a vacation when you feel bogged down by the daily grind. Taking yourself away from the hustle and bustle of everyday life allows more time to rest, relax, and be present in the moment.

Short vacations are a great way to break away from your everyday routines and raise your vibration. Whether a weekend trip to the countryside or a week-long stay in another country, these breaks give you space and time to enjoy yourself, relax, and enjoy the little things life offers.

Listen to Calming Music: When listening to music, you can access deep relaxation and energy. Calming music, like classical pieces or nature sounds, can help shift mood and raise your vibration instantly. Spending time with music is an opportunity for self-reflection and greater self-understanding.

Eat Healthy, Nourishing Foods: What you put into your body directly affects vibration and energy levels. Eating healthy, nutritious foods reduces stress and fatigue, leaving you feeling more energized and positive. A healthy diet full of fresh fruit, vegetables, superfoods, nuts, and seeds can help to restore balance to the body and mind.

Other healthy eating habits to include in your diet are avoiding processed and sugary foods, meal prepping, eating mindfully, and drinking plenty of water throughout the day.

Practicing Forgiveness and Mindfulness: Forgiveness is critical to raising positive vibration and letting go of negative energy. Practicing forgiveness can be difficult, but it is essential for releasing resentment or hurt you're holding onto. It can help heal relationships and bridge divides that have been created. Mindfulness is being present and aware in each moment without judgment. Practicing mindfulness helps you stay connected to yourself and the world around you instead of retreating into your thoughts or worries. It enhances the ability to experience joy and peace and be present for others.

Connecting with Kindness, Gratitude, and Abundance: Focusing on being kind to yourself and others helps raise vibration and energy levels. The same goes for cultivating gratitude and abundance. When expressing gratitude for small, everyday blessings, you can shift perception to appreciation and contentment. Focusing on the abundance already in your life helps you recognize the wealth of available resources. It opens new possibilities and opportunities and helps you lead a more meaningful life.

Engage in Activities that Bring Joy: Joy raises the vibration and is essential for a balanced life. Activities that bring joy, like dancing or playing a sport, can keep you connected with life. Remember, pleasure doesn't have to be big or grandiose; it can come in something as simple as making time for yourself every day.

Surround Yourself with Positive People: Surrounding yourself with positive people helps raise your vibration and increases self-confidence. When surrounded by those who support, encourage, and bring out the best in you, you feel more connected and fulfilled. Through shared experiences and conversations, you can learn from one another, challenge yourself and become the best version of yourself. Choose those who lift you up instead of bringing you down when selecting your inner circle.

Meditation is an incredibly powerful tool for tapping into your highest vibration. Meditating connects you with yourself deeper and accesses your inner wisdom. You can use meditation to clear negative energy or self-limiting beliefs holding you back so that you can move forward in life with greater clarity and purpose. Meditation helps restore balance and peace in the body, releasing tension or stress. Remember, raising your vibration is an ongoing practice; it requires dedication, commitment, and consistency to see lasting results. With patience and perseverance, you can reap the rewards of higher vibration, mentally and physically. So, take time today and tap into your highest vibration.

Chapter 5: The Healing Power of Reiki

Are you feeling stressed, uncertain, and not quite sure of how to make sense of the world we live in today? The Healing Power of Reiki may be just what you need. Many people have heard of it but don't understand how it works or why it's so powerful.

Reiki is an ancient healing practice that originated in Japan over 2000 years ago. It is based on the concept of "ki" or "chi," which is a life force energy existing in all living beings and connecting to the universe. Reiki channels this energy throughout the body to help it heal naturally. "Reiki" comes from two Japanese words, "rei," meaning universal, and "ki," meaning energy, translated as "universal life energy." It is based on the belief that all living things have an energy field or life force that must be balanced and harmonized for physical and emotional well-being. Reiki practitioners use their hands to channel positive energy into a person's body to promote relaxation and healing.

Reiki is an ancient healing practice that will allow you to cleanse your spirit.[28]

Reiki can be used as a preventative wellness measure and curative medicine - helping people with physical pain or emotional distress find relief without relying solely on medications or invasive treatments with unwanted side effects. It has benefited people with chronic conditions like fibromyalgia, arthritis, and mental health issues, like depression and anxiety, by helping them find greater balance within themselves while relieving their symptoms. Reiki can help increase the clarity of thought and aid better decision-making skills due to its ability to open up blocked energetic pathways inhibiting the ability to think clearly and make rational life decisions.

Origins

Reiki was first developed by a Japanese Buddhist monk, Mikao Usui, in 1922 after he experienced a spiritual awakening while meditating on Mount Kurama. During his time on the mountain, Usui felt a deep connection to ki's healing power and discovered how to use it for healing purposes. He spent several years studying and experimenting with this powerful form of healing before finally founding the Usui System of Reiki Healing.

Usui developed a system of five principles that form the basis of Reiki today. They are just for today, don't get angry, don't worry, be grateful, and do your best. In addition to these principles, three levels of Reiki practice require attunement by a teacher: Shoden (beginner level), Okuden (intermediate level), and Shinpiden (master level). Before moving on to the next level, the practitioner must demonstrate proficiency in each precedent level.

Since then, Reiki has continued to evolve and was brought to the Western world in the late 19th century by Dr. Chujiro Hayashi, who studied under Usui's teachings. In 1937, he opened his clinic, offering treatments to many people worldwide. In 1938, he introduced Reiki classes at universities so others could learn these techniques.

Today, Reiki is practiced worldwide by millions of people who believe using this technique helps them reach better mental, physical, and emotional balance. Practitioners use various hand positions above or on their client's bodies, focusing on their breath and allowing natural energy to flow freely through them while connecting deeply with their clients. During this process, they create an atmosphere filled with love and acceptance, allowing for deep healing within you and between humans who share this experience.

How Does Reiki Work?

Reiki balances the body's natural energies at its core through various hand placements called mudras. When these mudras are used correctly during a Reiki session, it helps restore the balance between the mind and body and enhance your overall well-being. During a typical session, practitioners use a light touch to direct positive energy into areas of the body that need it most - such as tension points or areas affected by illness or injury – while calming affirmations help release negative energy. Depending on individual needs, a session typically lasts 30 minutes to an hour.

Reiki practitioners believe illness can be caused by blocked energy pathways in the body. Using their hands to transfer life force energy into their client's bodies (channeled energy), they restore harmony within their client's systems and help them regain balance and wellness. The practitioner does not heal but instead channels the life force energy so that it can work on its recipient's behalf.

The practice consists of two main components:
1. **Hand placements** (or hand positions) on specific areas of the body corresponding with different parts of the body's energetic pathways.

2. **Intention setting** - this includes visualizing white light entering through your hands into your client's body while thinking positive thoughts for their well-being. Through these two aspects, practitioners can create an environment for healing and restoration within their client's bodies.

One example of Reiki healing is pain relief. When a person's muscles are tense due to physical or emotional stress, Reiki helps them relax by balancing the energies in their body's pathways. Reiki helps reduce inflammation, easing pain and discomfort associated with muscle tension and stiffness caused by injuries or illnesses, such as chronic fatigue syndrome or fibromyalgia. Many people report feeling energized after sessions because Reiki helps promote circulation throughout the body, providing beneficial nutrients while removing toxins deeper than most conventional treatments can reach.

Another example is helping people with anxiety disorders. Since Reiki works on physical and emotional levels, it can be extremely helpful for those with anxiety or depression. It helps restore balance throughout their mind, body, and spirit, promoting peace and relaxation instead of fear and worry. The client can move through difficult times more easily than if they were dealing with those emotions alone without help from outside sources like Reiki therapy sessions. In addition, many people find it helpful in treating sleep disorders. One common side effect is feeling relaxed enough so the client drifts into deep sleep quicker than normal after receiving a Reiki treatment. Practicing regularly with other healthy lifestyle choices like proper nutrition and exercise allows them to get better rest, positively impacting all other aspects of their life, including mental, emotional, physical, and spiritual wellbeing.

Reiki has been especially effective at helping stroke victims recover faster. Research studies have shown that clients who received regular Reiki treatments showed improved motor skills within weeks compared to those who did not receive this therapy combined with traditional medical interventions like occupational and physical therapies. It suggests that due to its ability to reduce inflammation and increase circulation throughout the body's systems, Reiki can speed up recovery times in certain cases.

Reiki has many benefits, including:
- Reducing stress and anxiety
- Promoting relaxation

- Improving sleep quality
- Increasing immunity boosts circulation
- Aiding muscle recovery
- Relieving pain and headaches
- Speeding up recovery times
- Providing clarity and insight into life paths

It's clear why so many people globally are turning toward this traditional healing modality nowadays rather than solely relying on Western medicine.

The 5 Reiki Principles

1. " Just for today, I will not be angry."

The first Reiki principle is "Just for today; I will not be angry." This notion emphasizes the importance of letting go of negative emotions and allowing yourself to live in the present moment. When you step back and observe your current situation, you can better understand how anger does not help you. Instead, it creates further tension by blocking energy flow and depriving you of thinking clearly.

When practicing this principle, you become aware of your thoughts and emotions before they cause harm. You become mindful of feelings and consider how each decision could potentially affect others. By taking a step back and looking at the bigger picture, you can better control emotions and behaviors and remain calm even in difficult situations or with people who trigger anger.

You can gradually work toward attaining inner peace by being mindful of thoughts, emotions, and actions while regularly practicing self-love. According to the first Reiki principle, "Just for today, I will not be angry," this belief eventually leads to living a more fulfilling life.

2. "Just for today, I will not worry."

The second Reiki principle encourages individuals to release their worries and focus on the present moment. This principle is "Just for today; I will not worry." This phrase helps people center on the present and let go of anxieties associated with overly worrying about the future or dwelling on the past.

When a person worries too much, it can lead to a negative mental state, and they can become trapped in their thoughts and struggles. It prevents them from fully embracing their lives and appreciating each moment as it occurs. Worrying can also cause physical stress, leading to headaches, stomachaches, fatigue, and other ailments complicating life. Reiki helps you break free from these patterns of worry by showing you how to be mindful of the present moment and take better care of yourself.

The phrase "Just for today, I will not worry" is an affirmation reminding you to stay in the present rather than ruminate on negative thoughts about the future or past events out of your control. Practicing this principle encourages individuals to live life intentionally instead of letting fear dictate their decisions or actions. It permits them to take time for themselves without feeling guilty or anxious, being kinder and gentler with themselves, so they have more energy for others.

3. "Just for today, I will do my work honestly."

The third Reiki principle is "Just for today; I will do my work honestly." This principle encourages being mindful of your intentions and motivations in your daily work. Taking ownership of your actions and being honest and ethical in everything you do is important. It enables you to build trust with others and ensure your actions positively impact those around you.

When doing honest work, remember to always act with integrity. It means being truthful in all interactions, taking responsibility for your mistakes, and not taking shortcuts or engaging in unethical practices like bribery or corruption. Your work will be of the highest quality. It will serve its intended purpose, maintaining a good reputation with those around you and building meaningful relationships based on mutual trust and respect.

Keeping your motivation pure when doing honest work is essential. You should strive to find joy in what you do rather than looking at it as a means toward an end or pursuing it solely out of greed or ambition. By working honestly, you help foster an environment of productivity, creativity, collaboration, and growth within yourself and those around you. You will inspire others to follow suit by setting a good example and demonstrating the value of hard work with integrity. This way, doing honest work creates a ripple effect by helping others reach their fullest potential.

4. "Just for today, be compassionate toward yourself and others."

The fourth Reiki principle is "Just for today, be compassionate toward yourself and others." This principle encourages self-compassion and kindness toward others, even when faced with difficulties. It calls you to set aside judgments and anger and focus on understanding others and your perspectives.

When practicing self-compassion, you accept your mistakes and shortcomings without excessive criticism or judgment. Additionally, self-compassion helps you work through difficult emotions healthily. When showing compassion toward others, you let go of feeling superior or inferior to them, recognizing that all people have flaws and no one is perfect. Compassion looks beyond these imperfections, helping you connect with one another more deeply.

Practicing self-compassion and compassion for others helps build resilience in times of adversity. When faced with challenging situations, you learn to respond with patience and understanding rather than judgment or anger and cope better with stressful life events. Furthermore, offering kindness and support to those in need benefits them and makes your life more meaningful.

5. "Just for today, I will be thankful for all my blessings."

The fifth Reiki principle is "Just for today; I will be thankful for all my blessings." This mantra encourages making a conscious effort to recognize and be grateful for your many blessings. By taking the time to appreciate what you have, you open up to the immense power of gratitude and abundance. Expressing thankfulness for life's simple pleasures, like a warm cup of tea or a sunny day, invites more of these moments into your life.

Gratitude helps cultivate positive emotions and relationships with others. Giving thanks and recognizing the good in those around you creates meaningful connections that could last a lifetime. Moreover, expressing gratitude allows you to better acknowledge daily successes and accomplishments, increasing satisfaction and motivation. It creates an attitude of abundance – not only material but spiritual abundance – which helps you to focus on what matters most.

Being thankful for all your blessings is a reminder that everything is fleeting and temporary. Life is full of ups and downs; it's important to recognize when times are good and savor them while they last. Gratitude helps keep life's minor problems in perspective by reminding you how much you have to be thankful for each day.

Can Reiki Be Self-Taught?

Reiki can be self-taught. However, many experts recommend working with an experienced practitioner if you are starting with this healing practice. Working with an experienced practitioner guides you on using Reiki for the best results and insight into what it means to become a Reiki practitioner. Nonetheless, some individuals have successfully learned how to do Reiki themselves through books, CDs, and other instructional materials available online or from specialty stores.

When practicing Reiki, remember everyone's experience is unique, and there is no one-size-fits-all approach to healing and balance. Each individual must find their way of connecting with the universal energy source when using this practice, whether through self-teaching methods or with an experienced Reiki master who helps guide their journey toward self-healing. Additionally, regular practice helps you become more attuned to your personal energy field, allowing you to effectively channel this energy for maximum benefit while treating yourself or others.

When learning Reiki, knowing it is all about energy flow is important. Therefore, developing an understanding of energy flow is key to mastering this technique. It can take time for your body to become attuned to the energy patterns of Reiki, but with proper training and commitment, you will eventually be able to manipulate this powerful force within yourself for healing purposes. Additionally, meditation practices benefit Reiki as they help put you in a relaxed state, allowing your body to open up more readily under its influence.

Anyone can learn to practice Reiki, whether they choose the traditional route by studying directly under a Master Teacher or teach themselves through books and other instructional resources available online and from specialty stores. Regardless, it takes dedication and commitment for someone seeking balance and wellness via this powerful modality to reap its full benefits, personally and professionally.

The Three Levels of Reiki

1. Shoden

Shoden is the first level of Reiki and the foundation of a Reiki practice. It introduces practitioners to Reiki and gives them a basic understanding of how it works and how to use it on themselves, other people, animals, plants, and objects.

During Shoden-level Reiki training, people learn more about energy healing, Reiki's history, its principles and etiquette (Rei-ki-ho), and the hand positions for self-treatment and treating others. Practitioners learn the power symbols used in treatments (Cho Ku Rei and Sei He Ki) and techniques for scanning the body for areas needing healing.

At this introductory level of learning, students are introduced to Dr. Mikao Usui's five principal teachings;

Just for today:
- Don't be angry
- Don't worry
- Be thankful
- Work hard
- Be kind to others

This teaching is integral to their training in understanding how to use Reiki and incorporate it into their daily lives.

The hands-on practice received at this level includes meditations where practitioners connect with their natural healing energy and Reiki methods on themselves by placing their hands in various positions on their body, sending Reiki energy through their hands. They receive instruction on how to treat others through touch or without touching by placing their hands a few inches away from someone's body while sending them healing energy.

In addition, practitioners are taught about personal boundaries when giving treatments and how to create a safe space for themselves and those they treat. By learning these basics during Shoden, practitioners develop a strong foundation serving them throughout future Reiki training levels.

2. Okuden

Okuden (intermediate level) is a level of Reiki building on the foundation of the Shoden (first level) teachings. It introduces more intricate concepts and practices, making practitioners more deeply attuned to their energy. This deeper understanding helps them to heal themselves and others better.

At the Okuden level, practitioners learn to use their life-force energy (ki) in healing processes. In addition, they learn techniques used to channel power from the universe into themselves and their clients, including focusing on a mental image or symbol when sending healing energy and focusing on an area of the body when performing treatments. They learn about the chakras and the auric field surrounding the body to identify healing or energizing areas.

Practitioners at the Okuden level will gain increased sensitivity to different energies and vibrations around them, allowing them to pick up on subtle clues during treatments indicating areas needing healing. At this stage, students learn techniques like long-distance healing to send Reiki energy over long distances without being physically present with their client.

The Okuden level is generally considered one of the most powerful levels of Reiki training available. Many practitioners feel it helps them to reach a new spiritual plane in their abilities. At this point, they connect with physical reality and unseen energies making up all aspects of existence – emotions, thoughts, and spirit. Mastering Okuden practitioners take responsibility for connecting with these higher spiritual energies and effectively moving forward in their chosen path toward self-mastery and personal growth.

3. Shinpiden

Shinpiden, known as the Master Level of Reiki, is the highest level of Reiki initiation. It involves a deep exploration of self-healing and energy awareness. At Shinpiden, practitioners receive three sacred symbols enhancing their healing capabilities and increasing their Reiki treatment power. This level allows practitioners to work with clients more profoundly, addressing deeper issues and blockages preventing them from living to their fullest potential.

At the Shinpiden level, practitioners gain an even greater understanding of using their Reiki energy combined with meditations, mantras, and affirmations for lasting results. They learn to identify energies hindering an individual's development or recovery from illness. Practitioners become masters of distance healing techniques, learning to connect with others spiritually regardless of physical proximity.

In addition to learning new symbols and techniques, Shinpiden practitioners are given specific tools to help them progress spiritually throughout life. These include communicating with higher guidance and creating powerful healing rituals or mantras to open up the pathways within themselves to tap into previously dormant spiritual powers. Practitioners are taught to access the Akashic Records containing all information about past lives and karmic patterns related to current life events.

Shinpiden students explore further aspects of Reiki, like spiritual counseling, kundalini activation, and soul retrieval, and advice on upholding spiritual boundaries when working with clients or conducting classes or workshops. Through this practice, they learn how best to work as conduits between the spirit world, natural elements, and humanity.

The journey taken at Shinpiden has been likened to completing a "spiritual apprenticeship" where a practitioner's true purpose is revealed. It helps them become conscious creators rather than victims of circumstances or limiting emotions and belief systems holding them back from achieving true happiness in this lifetime.

Chapter 6: Cleansing Energy with Reiki

Cleansing energy with Reiki is an incredibly powerful and research-backed tool to help improve physical, emotional, mental, and spiritual well-being. Your practitioner channels this special life energy into you to cleanse your aura and bring balance back into the body - allowing your cells access to more revitalizing vital force. This ancient practice is known to bring positive physical changes like increased energy levels, improved sleep patterns, and strengthened immune system functioning. Emotionally it can provide clarity of mind and less anxiety associated with stress. Mentally it offers better focus and clarity. Spiritually it nurtures peace, leading you toward your true life mission with unprecedented grace.

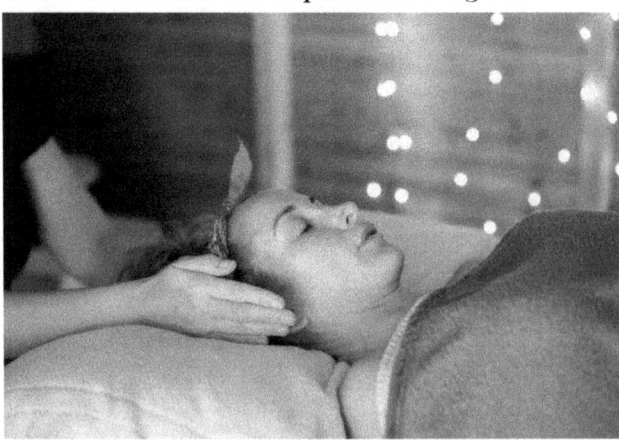

Reiki has the ability to cleanse any negative energy from your aura.[29]

How to Sense Energy through Reiki

Sensing energy is critical for Reiki practice, as practitioners can assess the energy flow in and around their clients. Understanding that everyone making up our world can feel or perceive subtle energies is important when beginning your journey into sensing energy. With practice, anyone can learn to detect and interpret this energy deeper.

The following exercises will help you become more proficient in sensing energy:

1. **Begin with an awareness meditation:** Sit comfortably in a quiet space, close your eyes, and focus on your breath. As thoughts arise, acknowledge them without judgment before gently returning your attention to your breathing. This exercise helps you become more mindful of your body and its sensations, allowing a heightened sense of awareness.

2. **Intentional grounding:** *Grounding* is connecting with the Earth's energy, helping you become more centered and connected to yourself and your environment. While seated or standing, place both feet firmly on the ground and shift your focus to this connection between yourself and the Earth. Visualize roots coming out of each foot as they travel down into the ground below. Once you feel connected, take deep breaths and relax into this feeling of stability.

3. **Scanning for energy:** Find a comfortable seated position or lie down in bed before slowly scanning your body for feelings that arise. You may feel sensations like warmth, tingling, or vibrations as you move your focus. If something stands out, pay closer attention to that area. As you do this exercise more often, you will recognize more subtle reactions and gain greater insight into the energy field surrounding your body.

4. **Connecting with others:** Stand or sit in a relaxed position with the person in front of you to practice sensing another person's energy field. Once connected with their presence through eye contact, release all expectations and become aware of feelings or impressions that arise within you during this connection. As time passes during this exchange, be open to the information you receive and pay attention to subtle changes in the energy you are sensing.

These simple steps will help you better understand the energy within yourself and others and become more proficient in using Reiki for healing purposes. Remember, practice makes perfect, so be patient with yourself as you explore this new realm of energy. With consistent effort and dedication, you can unlock the mysteries of Reiki energy.

Level 1-2 Reiki Techniques for Clearing Unwanted Energy from the Body

Pre Reiki Rituals

- **Reiki Attunements**

Reiki attunements, known as initiations, are essential in Reiki training. During an attunement ceremony, the Reiki practitioner enters a state of heightened receptivity so that they are open and receptive to Reiki's energy. Essentially, they are "tuned in" to the life force energy flowing through all living things. This tuning-in process enables them to access and transmit this powerful healing energy more easily and accurately.

- **Using Reiki Symbols**

Reiki symbols are integral to the Reiki healing practice and can help further deepen its effectiveness. They open and balance the energy channels in the body, allowing a more efficient flow of healing energy. The specific symbols used depend on the practitioner's tradition but typically include Cho Ku Rei, Sei He Ki, Hon Sha Ze Sho Nen, Dai Ko Myo, and Raku.

Cho Ku Rei is a symbol of power, protection, and grounding throughout Reiki sessions. It is believed to clear negative energy from an aura or environment and strengthen the connection to their higher self.

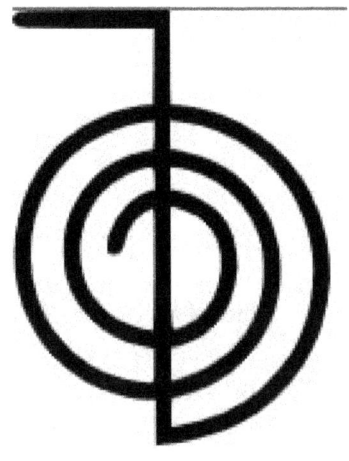

Cho Ku Rei.[80]

Sei He Ki helps promote mental clarity while aiding in emotional healing. It is a particularly powerful symbol for helping process emotions a person has difficulty working through without assistance.

Sei He Ki.[81]

Hon Sha Ze Sho Nen assists in distance healing by creating an energetic bridge between two people so they benefit from a session, even if they are not physically with each other.

Hon Sha Ze Sho Nen.[82]

Dai Ko Myo represents spiritual enlightenment and helps you to open up a deeper understanding of yourself.

Raku encourages growth and transformation in life by viewing yourself from a place of non-judgmental acceptance.

Using these symbols during practice can help amplify the power of Reiki and help clear energy blocks in the body or mind. They are used before starting a session or as needed throughout to break up stagnant energies getting in the way of successful healing. When these symbols are used with intention, their effectiveness increases exponentially, so focus on them when invoking these special tools in your practice.

Dai Ko Myo.[88]

Steps for Cleansing Unwanted Energies
Reiki Breath and Visualization Technique

The Reiki Breath technique is a gentle and effective way of clearing unwanted energy from your body or another's. It is a simple yet powerful tool for clearing obstructions in the body in just a few minutes. Here are the steps to guide you through this technique:

1. Sit or lie down comfortably with your feet resting flat on the floor or ground. You can close or open your eyes, whichever feels more comfortable.
2. Take several deep breaths to relax, become aware of your intuition, and visualize a white light entering your body. Sink into this visualization and focus on feeling love and peace radiating throughout your being.
3. Once you have taken several deep breaths, imagine the negative energy in your body being released through your breath - thoughts, emotions, physical pain, etc. See this energy evaporating from you

until it has completely dissipated from your being.

4. After releasing your negative energy, you can extend Reiki healing to others. Visualize a white light emanating from the center of your heart chakra and extending outward like fingers around someone's body whom you want to help heal - even if they are not with you physically - until it envelopes them in a loving embrace of light and warmth. Use other colors of light depending on the healing.

5. Allow yourself to imagine negative energy or obstructions within their bodies releasing through their breath. At the same time, they, too, take deep breaths - see them in their relaxed state with no pain or discomfort before slowly opening your eyes, feeling refreshed and revitalized.

Reiki Hand Position Technique

The next step is using the Reiki hand position technique, a powerful way to clear unwanted energy from the body.

1. After completing the visualization, take a few deep breaths to become fully present and relaxed.

2. When you feel ready, place your hands in various positions on the body - like the abdomen, chest, back, or head. With each position, take time to sense sensations that arise. Do not try to control these sensations but allow them to move through you. Move slowly and feel the energy entering your hands.

3. Once you have placed your hands in each position, gently move them in small circles or waves on the area for around 3-5 minutes. It helps clear out unwanted energy from the person's body, allowing space for healing energies to enter.

4. Furthermore, it is important not to apply too much pressure while moving your hands; instead, allow yourself to be guided by whatever feels right at each moment. Trust that Reiki knows how to balance the energies of the person's body best.

- **Hand Positions for Self-Cleansing**

The Prayer Position: Simply bring both hands together in front of your heart center. Press your palms firmly against each other and your fingertips pointing toward the sky. It creates a powerful energetic connection between both hands, acting as a bridge between the physical and the spiritual world, allowing you to draw out stuck energy which may be obstructing your energy flow. This position is ideal for anyone looking to create balance within their system or open up blocked chakras.

The Open Palm Position: Sit with your spine straight and extend both arms directly out in front of you at shoulder height, palms facing outward. Take slow deep breaths while visualizing yourself, sending healing light from your fingertips into the environment. As you exhale, imagine negative or stuck energy being pulled out through your palms and back into the environment where it will be transmuted away from your system forever. This position helps expand your energetic fields while providing protection from outside influences that might otherwise interfere with your vibrations.

The Palms Down Position: Sit comfortably with arms extended forward at shoulder height, palms facing down toward the ground beneath you. Imagine roots growing out from each fingertip into the Earth below, where they can draw in nurturing energies while simultaneously drawing out heavy or stagnant energy built up over time within your system. This exercise helps connect deeply to Mother Earth's nourishing embrace while promoting grounding and stability on all mental, emotional, and physical levels.

- **Hand Position for Cleansing Another Person's Energies**

You can use numerous hand positions to clear unwanted energy from another person's body. Each position facilitates different aspects of the energy-clearing process, from focusing on specific areas to creating a more comprehensive clearing effect.

One of the most basic hand positions for energy cleansing is placing one or both hands hovering an inch over the person's chakras or energy centers. It helps clear out stagnant or stuck energy in those areas. Visualizing a particular color -pink, blue, or green - associated with healing and cleansing as you use this technique can be beneficial.

Another popular hand position requires cupping your hands around the person's head and shoulders while taking deep breaths together. Combine this technique with visualizing a healing light entering through your palms and into your body. This technique helps create overall balance and well-being.

Use your hands to massage tension points in the person's body, such as their back, neck, and shoulders. Gently massaging these areas helps release built-up stress and tension, allowing more positive energy to flow through them unhindered. You could add soothing aromatherapy oils for extra relaxation benefits.

Grounding

The Reiki grounding technique to clear unwanted energy is creating a grounding cord.

Take a few moments to concentrate and refocus.

1. Close your eyes and take several deep breaths. Feel your feet on the floor and imagine being connected to the Earth's energy through its core.
2. Visualize a grounding cord extending from the base chakra, at the base of your spine, down into the earth below you. This cord should be visible in whatever form or color feels natural; some people imagine it as a thick rope, others as an electrical wire.
3. Focus on feeling connected with this energy so that all excess or unwanted energies can be pulled out through this cord and back into the earth, transmuted into light and love.
4. Once you have established your grounding cord, place your hands over the area of concern (yourself or another person) for about three minutes. Stay present in your breath throughout this process. It is important to stay aware of what is happening within you and in the environment around you.
5. If needed, silently ask for guidance from higher sources or spiritual beings offering assistance during this session.

After completing step five, slowly release the tension held throughout this process by slowly exhaling until feeling more relaxed before beginning future steps in this clearing process. It is beneficial to thank spiritual entities who assisted you during the session before finishing with self-care, like a cup of tea or walking outside in nature.

Final Release

The final release is the final step in cleansing unwanted energies from your or another's body. Take a few deep breaths and ground yourself, visualizing excess or unwanted energies leaving the body through a white light. It is essential to give gratitude for the Reiki healing and thank the Reiki energy for aiding in cleansing unwanted energies, as this could be a crucial part of spiritual healing.

Next, moving into a relaxed state and letting yourself settle into stillness is important. If desired, take this time to reflect on your experience and write down what you experienced during the healing process journals. Your journals will allow you to reflect on your journey toward spiritual growth and development, so take some time to recognize what you have learned during the process of releasing energy.

Finally, end your session with meditation or contemplation. Focus on your breathing patterns and allow yourself to be surrounded by stillness while holding positive thoughts. Do not forget to remain grateful for all you have learned during this journey - self-reflection can lead to a further understanding of innermost thoughts, desires, beliefs, and values. You will feel energized or refreshed when you finish. Whatever emotions you feel in that moment are valid and should be embraced fully before returning to reality with a renewed awareness.

Can Reiki Cleanse Unblocked Chakras?

A Reiki cleanse is a great way to unblock chakras. Reiki combines touch and meditation to help bring balance and harmony to the body's energy systems. During a Reiki cleanse, the practitioner uses their hands in specific positions over the chakras corresponding with each chakra's energy centers. The practitioner allows the energy flow to be released from these chakra points, clearing blockages or disruption, using the healing power of Reiki's universal life force energy throughout the entire body, including the chakras.

The chakras are essential for physical and emotional health, as they control the ability to connect energetically. When one or more chakras become blocked, it can cause a number of issues ranging from physical pain and illness to mental health problems like anxiety and depression. A Reiki cleanse can help clear obstructions built up over time while restoring proper balance throughout all seven chakras. It helps clear negative emotions and feelings trapped within you due to life experiences or traumas, so you can move forward more positively with renewed energy and joy.

Reiki is a powerful healing modality facilitating physical, emotional, mental, and spiritual well-being. It helps individuals reconnect with their deepest essence - their true self - increasing overall peace and joy to live an empowered life filled with purposeful intention. Unblocking energetic blocks within the chakras through regular Reiki cleanses individuals and creates a foundation for lasting health on all levels; mind, body, soul, and spirit.

Chapter 7: To Smudge or Not to Smudge

You don't know what to do. To smudge or not to smudge? This is an important decision, as smudging is a powerful spiritual practice. Smudging is burning sacred herbs and resins, like sage, cedar, sweetgrass, and lavender, to purify and cleanse the energy of a space. Many cultures have specific traditions for smudging, often involving prayer or other rituals. For example, in some Native American cultures, sweetgrass braids are lit and used for smudging to release the sacred plant's positive energy into the air. Whatever your reason for wanting to cleanse an area spiritually, smudging may be just the thing.

Smudging is a process that has been used by many cultures for different spiritual purposes.[84]

Is Smudging Closed Practice or a Cultural Appropriation?

Smudging, a sacred practice of burning herbs or resins to purify a space, has been popularized in recent years. This practice is often associated with Native American cultures. Many spiritual and new-age practitioners consider it a closed practice, meaning it should only be used by those within the culture with the right knowledge and understanding of its importance.

In addition to being considered a closed practice, some claim that smudging has become an example of cultural appropriation (when one culture takes elements from another without permission or understanding the original context). It includes adopting symbols from other cultures or attempting to pass off traditional practices as their own. For example, many people learn about smudging from books, TV shows, and movies rather than through traditional teachings without full knowledge of its spiritual significance and implications.

The controversy surrounding smudging has grown over the past few years as more non-natives attempt to use it for their spiritual practices without fully understanding its history and significance. For example, celebrities like Gwyneth Paltrow have posted photos on social media performing smudges in their homes. It may be harmless enough at face value, but if done without proper respect for the tradition, it can be seen as appropriative behavior.

However, not all non-natives engaging in smudging do it out of disrespect - many individuals find real spiritual benefit in its use - but even those with good intentions can cause harm if they do not properly respect the traditions. When engaging with smudging, it's crucial for anyone who is not part of the culture to take time to research its history, understand its significance within Native American contexts, ask permission when appropriate, and give credit where due when sharing information. It helps prevent the practice from being appropriated or trivialized by those outside its traditions and ensures native voices are heard when discussing issues around these spiritual practices.

The Difference between Smudging and Smoke Cleansing

Smudging and smoke cleansing are ancient spiritual rituals used for centuries to cleanse and protect people, places, and objects. While both use smoke to purify, the two practices have some distinct differences.

Smudging is a ritual practice dating back thousands of years and is most commonly associated with Native American culture. It uses a bundle of sage, sweetgrass, cedar, tobacco, or other dried herbs to create an incense-like substance. This smudge is lit until it creates smoke, which cleanses the area or person of negative energy. Smudging is often used for prayer, meditation, and connecting with the spirit world.

On the other hand, smoke cleansing or fumigation has its roots in many ancient cultures, including Greek, Roman, and African traditions. It involves burning specific herbs like frankincense or sandalwood over charcoal tablets to produce a large amount of fragrant smoke. This smoke purifies an environment or object by clearing out stagnant energy or negative influences while simultaneously healing emotional wounds and restoring balance in the body's energy field.

Smudging and smoke cleansing both use fragrant smoke to purify an area or object, but they differ primarily in their origin stories and ingredients when performing the rituals. Smudging often uses bundles of dried herbs, whereas smoke cleansing utilizes specific herbs like frankincense or sandalwood burned over charcoal tablets. Smudging typically serves spiritual purposes related to prayer or connecting with the spirit world. Smoke cleansing primarily focuses on healing emotional wounds and restoring balance in energy fields rather than invoking spiritual guidance.

Benefits of Smoke Cleansing

Smoke cleansing is an ancient practice used by many indigenous cultures and Shamans for centuries. They believe it is a powerful way to clear negative energy and create balance and harmony in a space. Smoke cleansing involves burning natural herbs such as sage, cedar, sweetgrass, copal, lavender, or palo santo, which release fragrant smoke into the air. As the smoke travels through the air, it has the power to cleanse a space of negative energies, creating positive feelings and raising vibration.

One of the greatest benefits of smoke cleansing is its ability to help reduce stress and anxiety, usually through the calming effects of its smell. The pleasant aroma released by burning herbs like sage or cedar helps promote relaxation and calmness in the body and mind. Additionally, this smell can inspire creativity due to its potential ability to heighten your senses.

Smoke cleansing has also been proven to have antiseptic properties. It can effectively purify the air in a room with viruses or bacteria causing respiratory issues or illnesses like colds and flu. Therefore, it is an ideal way to disinfect indoor spaces without using harmful chemicals or sprays. Furthermore, smoke cleansing can improve concentration due to its soothing aroma helping to foster a relaxing atmosphere, perfect for studying or working on tasks requiring greater focus and attention span.

Another key benefit of smoke cleansing is its spiritual aspect. It is believed that when practiced in sacred ceremonies, besides clearing built-up negative energies, it attracts positive intentions from the universe, allowing you to manifest your desires more easily. In addition, by focusing on each herb during your ritual, you can connect with its medicinal properties, which are healing agents for physical, emotional, and mental health issues like inflammation and depression.

Smoke cleansing is beneficial because it encourages mindful presence during rituals, actively engaging all five senses; sight (seeing), sound (hearing), smell (smelling), taste (tasting), and touch (feeling). This mindful practice helps bring awareness into your daily life, helping you stay connected with your surroundings while developing greater self-awareness along the journey.

Many incredible benefits are associated with smoke cleansing:
- Reducing stress levels and anxiety
- Improving concentration
- Purifying air
- Drawing positive intentions from the universe
- Aiding physical, emotional, and mental health healing
- Encouraging mindfulness

It is an invaluable ritual for anyone seeking spiritual growth and personal development.

Types of Smoke Cleansing

A herb combination for smoke cleansing is the traditional Native American smudging practice, which uses four main herbs; white sage, sweetgrass, cedar, and lavender. White sage spiritually cleanses an area by driving out negative energy. Sweetgrass helps bring in positive energy. Cedar purifies a space, protects against bad luck, and promotes longevity. Lavender helps promote relaxation and peace of mind. By burning these herbs together, the smoke created can cleanse a person or room of negative energies and protect them from harm.

Another herb combination often used for smoke cleansing is palo santo wood, from South America, where it's traditionally used in shamanic healing ceremonies. When burned, this wood produces a fragrant smoke, which helps purify an environment by reducing negative energy, stress, and anxiety, promoting calmness, peace, and enlightenment. Palo santo wood helps people connect with their higher selves during meditation or prayer rituals by aiding in reaching deeper levels of consciousness.

Finally, many cultures worldwide use herbal mixtures for smoke-cleansing purposes, including frankincense and myrrh from Ethiopia and Copal from Guatemala, among others. Frankincense was traditionally burned as incense to cleanse spaces and ward off evil spirits or bad luck. The aroma of burning this resin helps clear away negative energy, allowing those present to feel relaxed, comforted, and safe in their surroundings. Myrrh has long been associated with religious ceremonies due to its strong aromatic scent, and it aids in connecting with a higher power. Burning this resin encourages reverence, creating an atmosphere conducive to meditation or prayer. Copal is another tree resin whose smoke has been used for spiritual purification ceremonies since ancient times. Its fragrant aroma is known to drive away negativity, simultaneously protecting against evil influences.

How to Create Your Smudge Stick

Creating your smudge stick is quite straightforward, but it requires patience and a good amount of research. Before you start, double-check if the herbs you use are safe to burn. Some plants contain oils or toxins that can be dangerous when burned in an enclosed space. Additionally, be mindful of allergic reactions – some people are sensitive to certain plants.

When picking herbs for your smudge stick, opt for more accessible herbs, such as white sage (*Salvia apiana*), cedar (*Juniperus virginiana*), mugwort (*Artemesia vulgaris*), lavender (*Lavandula angustifolia*), and rosemary (*Rosmarinus officinalis*). These herbs have an array of benefits, from protection and cleansing to healing.

Here are the steps to make your smudge stick once you've chosen your herbs:

1. Gather long branches or stems of herbs and bundle them together with a string. Leave enough space between each herb so air can circulate throughout the bundle.
2. Securely tie the string into a knot at one end, then wrap it around the middle of the bundle several times before tying it off again on the other end.
3. To dry the smudge stick, hang it in a warm, well-ventilated area like a garage or porch for two weeks. Turn it over every other day so the herbs will dry evenly.
4. When your smudge stick is completely dry, it is ready to burn. You can light it directly with a match, or if you want more control over the smoke, place a bowl of sand and charcoal underneath the smudge stick.

When burning your smudge stick, you must keep an eye on the embers and put out any that are too big. Never leave the burning herb unattended for long periods because of fire hazard risks. Remember to dispose of the ashes properly in a metal container filled with sand or water when the ritual is finished.

Creating your smudge stick can be a rewarding and spiritual experience, as it is an ancient ritual used to ward off negative energy, cleanse the home, and bring in positive vibes. However, it's important to research beforehand and ensure your herbs are safe to burn. If you want to learn more about various herbs and plants for this purpose, take a peek at the chapter glossary of herbs at the end of this book for further information.

Types of Smudge Sticks

There are many different smudge sticks, each with unique properties and uses.

1. **White Sage Smudge Stick:** White sage is a common smudge stick for cleansing and purifying. It is usually burned as incense or added to other herbs for deeper cleansing. This sage has a strong, pungent smell and is used to clear the air of negative energy.
2. **Cedar Smudge Stick:** Cedar is another popular choice for smudging and has similar purposes as white sage. The cedar's scent is earthy and sweet, helping to promote grounding and safety in the home or office space. In some Native American tribes, cedar was used to bring prosperity and success into the home.
3. **Mugwort Smudge Stick:** Mugwort is less commonly known than white sage or cedar but has been used in various cultures since ancient times. The smoke of burning mugwort carries healing properties to help with lucid dreaming and healing emotional trauma. It protects from harmful energies when burned indoors or outdoors.
4. **Palo Santo Smudge Stick:** *Palo santo* comes from South America and is made from fragrant wood pieces of trees found in Peru, Ecuador, Mexico, and Guatemala. The smoke of burning palo santo has spiritual cleansing powers to help clear negative energy from space when burned regularly. It has a more pleasant aroma than other smudge sticks, making it perfect for aromatherapy and spiritual cleansing rituals.
5. **Sweetgrass:** Sweetgrass is an herb native to North America that's often used in sacred ceremonies because it invokes gratitude and positivity in those who experience its fragrance. Sweetgrass helps clear away negative energy and brings blessings into the environment where it's being burned.

How to Cleanse Yourself

Start by creating an environment of peace and tranquility. You can achieve this through essential oils, like lavender or chamomile, dimming the lights, playing soft music, burning incense, or other measures that help create a calming atmosphere.

Next, take deep breaths to relax your body and mind. As you breathe in, imagine all positive energy entering your body, leaving you feeling relaxed and refreshed. As you breathe out, imagine releasing all the negativity away from you. Continue until you are in a completely tranquil state.

Now, it is time to open your aura and release all the stagnant energy. Recite the affirmation: *"I open my aura and release all stagnation within it."* Visualize a powerful light radiating from the center of your chest, slowly expanding and cleansing your energy field. Do this until you feel your aura is completely clear of negative energy.

The next step is to recite positive affirmations or prayers. You can do these silently or aloud, depending on what resonates with you best. Some examples of positive affirmations include, *"I am worthy of love and happiness"* or *"My life is full of abundance and gratitude."* Some traditional prayers are The Lord's Prayer, The Hail Mary, or Psalm 23.

In addition to affirmations and prayers, using sound can cleanse and balance the energy fields. Examples of sounds to help with cleansing include singing bowls, tuning forks, bells, or clapping hands. These tools vibrate your energy field, allowing stagnant energy to dissipate.

Herbal remedies are popular for cleansing yourself spiritually. Many herbs have properties to help open up the heart chakra, allowing for love, acceptance, and healing to enter your life. Common herbs used in cleansing include lavender, sage, rosemary, jasmine, and mint. You can use these herbs by burning them during meditation or ritual practices, drinking them as teas or infusions, or carrying them around with you when you need a reminder that you are on a spiritual journey.

Finally, closing your aura once you're finished with the cleansing ritual is important. Take deep breaths and visualize a powerful light radiating from the center of your chest, slowly shrinking until all your energy is fully contained within it. Affirm, *"My aura is closed, and I am protected,"* as you do this visualization. It helps keep negative energies away, so you remain in an open state for positive energies.

Following these simple steps, you can successfully cleanse yourself and remain in a state of peace and positivity. Remember to include positive affirmations and prayers, and use sound to maximize the effects. Lastly, take time to appreciate yourself for participating in this cleansing ritual and express gratitude for everything you have achieved.

Regularly cleanse yourself to benefit from the inner peace and clarity of releasing negativity and inviting more positivity into your life.

How to Cleanse Your Home

Cleansing your home is vital in spiritual practice. Cleansing can help clear stagnant energy and bring in fresh, positive vibrations. It helps create safety, peace, and comfort in your home. Follow these steps to cleanse your home:

1. **Clear the air:** Open the windows and doors to allow fresh air inside. Light incense or sage sticks fill the space with cleansing smoke. If you have essential oils available, you can use them, too. Mix two drops of jasmine, lavender, and lemon essential oil in a diffuser for a soothing scent with purifying benefits.

2. **Create a mantra:** Focus on the intention of clearing away negative energy and inviting positive vibrations into your home. Create a simple mantra you can repeat to yourself, such as "*My home is full of love and light*" or "*All negativity be gone from my space.*"

3. **Visualize:** Take a few moments to close your eyes and visualize all the energies in your home released through the open windows and doors. Imagine white or gold light entering your home with fresh air and filling every corner of your space with peacefulness.

4. **Use sound:** Singing bowls, chimes, tuning forks, drums, or other instruments are great tools for cleansing spaces energetically. You can use traditional chants like Om and the Gayatri Mantra to bless your home with positivity.

5. **Pray:** Offer a prayer or affirmation of gratitude and ask for protection from negative energies. Light a candle and focus on sending love into your home, then blow out the flame to signal the completion of this cleansing stage.

6. **Cleanse crystals:** Crystals have special properties that energetically cleanse homes, so if you have them in your space, it's important to clear them periodically. Place each crystal in sea salt overnight and rinse it off the next day. This will help remove the buildup of energy absorbed over time.

7. **Focus on self-care**: Take the time to treat yourself kindly. Spend time in meditation or relax and connect with your breath. It will help you remain grounded and centered after cleansing your

home.
8. **Seal it:** To finish your ritual, smudge around the four corners of each room with incense or sage smoke, then seal the doorways with salt to keep negative energy out and protect your sacred space. You can use a quartz crystal in each corner for added protection.
9. **Give Thanks:** Take a few moments to thank the universe for all you have and the cleansing energy within your home. Feel free to add prayers, affirmations, sounds, essential oils, or other items that feel right for your space. When you have finished, take one final deep breath and relax into the positive energy in your cleansed space.

How to Cleanse a Negative Object

Cleansing an object can be a powerful way to reclaim the energy and space within your home. It is important to do this ritual to protect yourself from negative energies that might have been left behind. Cleansing an object uses various methods, such as prayers, affirmations, sounds, essential oils, smudging with herbs or incense, visualization with or without candles, or chanting. Here are step-by-step instructions for cleansing an object:

1. Start by physically cleaning the object. Make sure it is free of dirt and dust before you move on to other cleansing techniques.
2. Select a prayer or affirmation that resonates with you and speak aloud while focusing on the object Examples of prayers or affirmations; "*I cleanse this object of all energy that does not belong to me,*" "*I fill this space with positive, loving energy.*"
3. Use a sound tool like a drum or crystal singing bowl and create a vibration around the object. It will help release the negative energy attached to it.
4. Smudge the object with herbs or incense, such as sage, cedar, sweetgrass, or palo santo wood. As you smudge around the object, focus on releasing the negative energies left behind and invite peace and love.
5. Visualize the object surrounded by a white light or energy field protecting it from unwanted energies. You can use candles around the object to help create an inviting space.

6. Chant mantras or words of power that are meaningful to you while focusing on the object. It will help raise its vibration and invite positive energy into your home.
7. Place drops of essential oils, such as lavender, frankincense, or sandalwood, on the object for added protection and cleansing benefits.
8. Finally, thank your spiritual source for helping cleanse this object and set a clear intention of how you want to use it in the future.

By following these cleansing techniques, you can be confident the object has been cleansed of negative energy and is ready for use in your home. Remember, stay mindful of how you use the object to prevent unwanted energies from returning to your space. May peace, love, and light be with you.

Chapter 8: Spiritual Baths for Cleansing and Protection

Baths have been part of spiritual practices since ancient times. They were known for their healing, cleansing, and protective properties and their ability to relieve stress and anxiety symptoms and improve overall well-being. People in ancient times felt drawn to water subconsciously. They understood that water was essential for survival and acknowledged its spiritual healing properties. Bathing was a regular custom in Ancient Greece, India, Israel, and Egypt. In most of these cultures, bathing was known as purification by water, especially if bathed in salt water. The most primitive forms of this practice included visiting springs known for healing practice and submerging in water as an expression of devotion to their faith. Drawing on a bath with stones and salt was developed later as part of spiritual pursuits. The added salt or rock water enhanced the water's cleansing properties, and people gladly took advantage of it.

If this is the first time you've heard of a spiritual bath, you aren't alone. However, many people take spiritual baths before even realizing they've existed. For example, if you took a bath longer than necessary to get clean, you've already stepped into this spiritual practice. If you prefer baths over showers, you already know nothing compares to soaking in a hot, soothing bath after a busy day. Many people enjoy taking their time reading, listening to music, or sipping a glass of wine while soaking. They might even light a candle or two. They let the water and the stillness of the moment relax them. However, spiritual baths are slightly different. They require an intention and an active approach to relaxing. Otherwise, you cannot focus on your intent, and your bath rituals won't be as effective as when you channel your intention. The key to performing this spiritual exercise is knowing what you expect from your time in the water. As you submerge your entire body, your intention channels the energies you want to work on. Therefore, lie down and soak yourself well while repeating your intentions.

The best characteristic of spiritual baths is you can always put your spin on them. This chapter provides instructions for baths for spiritual cleansing and protection, but you're free to alter them to your liking. You can infuse them with other preferred spiritual tools to boost the effectiveness of your intention and nourish it until its manifests into reality.

The Purpose of Spiritual Baths

A spiritual bath is a magnificent way to refresh your body, mind, and soul. You can supply your body, mind, and soul with healing energy, allowing them to protect you from harmful influences. You've probably noticed that you feel different after taking a regular bath than you did before - your sense of rejuvenation and calmness goes beyond your body. Due to their ingredients, spiritual baths can amplify this feeling. These ingredients often contain unique energies or compounds affecting your energy. They have different purposes, which you can use in a spiritual bath with specific intent.

The primary purpose of spiritual baths is to give yourself time to reflect on the sensation enveloping your body and those that go beyond. During a spiritual bath, inspect your emotions in the present moment. Taking the time and space to ground yourself enables you to identify areas in your body, mind, and spirit that could benefit from energetic healing.

While you examine the problematic areas, seek inspiration for working on them through other means. Therefore, spiritual baths are not only cleansing and protective, but they're also centering and motivating. They can take you closer to nature and be grateful for its gifts, including the water and all the natural ingredients in your bath.

Another purpose of spiritual baths is to balance the chakras, which heal your mind, body, and soul. Clearing blockages from the chakras contributes to their healthy function and ability to prevent illnesses and injuries.

The Benefits of Spiritual Baths

A spiritual bath can have different benefits depending on your ingredients and intention. Typically, spiritual baths purify one energetic field and cleanse the body, mind, and spirit. Other benefits include:

- **Lessening the effects of external stimuli:** In this fast-paced world, you are constantly bombarded with information. The environments you move in, the people you deal with, and the entertainment you consume are all packed with stimuli affecting your energies. Spiritual baths can help lower the energy imprint of those influences disrupting your balance.

- **Relax the nervous system:** Many ingredients in spiritual baths can soothe irritated nerves, restore hormone balance affecting the nervous system, and reduce the effects of negative emotions. It has a wholesome influence on your overall health. After a stressful day, you can take a bath to tune out all your worries and enjoy a soothing atmosphere.

- **Flushing out toxins:** Soaking in the bathtub with salt water or other ingredients with antioxidative effects is as effective as drinking detox drinks. Moreover, a bath takes less time to prepare and has less potential for unwanted effects on your body. By spending only 20 minutes in a bathtub, you'll flush out all the toxins in your body and promote your well-being.

- **Creating the perfect atmosphere for contemplation:** Since you're already relaxing and cleansing in your bathtub, you can use the time for a little reflective investigation of yourself. You can ponder your intention or think about your goals and desires; the latter practice is excellent for establishing a connection between your intuition and your spiritual self. You can use any exercise to gain more self-awareness and reveal your innermost needs.

- **Purifying the energetic body:** Spiritual baths have a therapeutic effect on balancing your subtle energies. They replace stagnant or harmful energy with positive vibes and raise your vibrations. Salts, crystals, and essential oils are essential for cleansing your energetic body. Essential oils will help you replace the flushed-out energy with renewed energy, especially if you spend at least 25-30 minutes soaking and relaxing in the tub.

How to Take a Spiritual Bath

There are no instructions on how to take a spiritual bath. However, you should always use an intention and ingredients that fit your current needs. Regardless of your goal, you can take a few steps to make your baths more effective. Infusing your bath with the most appropriate intention is crucial, granting you a greater experience.

Instructions:
1. **Ensure your bathtub is clean before you take a bath.** Otherwise, the residual negative energy can interfere with the bath rituals, reducing their effectiveness. Whether you want cleansing, protection, or healing, the number one rule is to start with a clean slate. Cleaning the bathtub and the surrounding area helps eliminate harmful influences from your bathroom and allows your baths to take full effect.
2. **You can play music.** It can be meditation music or music that helps you relax and adds to the bath's spiritual cleansing and protection benefits. Alternatively, you can listen to a guided meditation while you soak. Or, if you're confident enough, you can sing before and after the bath. The latter helps clear the space from negative energies that have exited your body, mind, and spirit while soaking.
3. **Stay unplugged.** The ability to listen to music or sounds doesn't mean you should be on your phone or use other electronic devices while soaking. Place any device playing the audio as far away from your reach as possible to remain "unplugged."
4. **Set a clear intent.** Whether you want your energetic pathways cleansed, resolve negative situations, cleanse your body, mind, and spirit, or attract positive influences into your life, define it clearly before you prepare for your bath.
5. **Take your time** reflecting on how you feel before and after taking a bath. Not all cleansing baths work for everyone. To see if a particular bath works for you, acknowledge what you need help with and compare your results to how you felt before taking it.
6. **When using essential oils and herbs, you must be familiar with their effects.** Not all herbs and oils are safe for everyone,

particularly on your skin, and only use those recommended for baths. If you notice an adverse reaction, stop using them in your baths.

Bath to Reinforce Your Psychic Defenses

This is the right bath for you if you feel vulnerable to negative influences and need empowerment to attract positive energy. It will reinforce your psychic defenses, helping you ward off negative energies and keep your chakras balanced and healthy. It uses Himalayan salt, known for its ability to deter negative energy, drawing it away from the body and the toxins causing the negative energy accumulation. If you have this option, take a bath next to an open window at full moon to let the moonlight bless you while you soak.

Ingredients:
- Blessed water (or water charged with spiritual energy from crystals, the moon, etc.)
- Essential oils or other plant-based scents
- Candles
- Herbs - fresh or dry
- Incense
- Crystals
- Himalayan salt
- Tea bags
- Moonlight (optional)
- Relaxing music (optional)

Instructions:
1. Set the appropriate mood in your bathroom. Light several candles around the bathtub and turn off the artificial lights. You can light incense and turn on relaxing music.
2. Consider your intention. Think about what you want to achieve from this bath and how you can help your mind and spirit improve your psychic defenses. Focus on your intention.
3. Fill your bathtub with water at the appropriate temperature and add the cleansing ingredients. You can use as many or as few

as you like.
4. When the tub is filled, get in the water. As you enjoy soaking, concentrate on taking deep breaths. Feel how the air moves through your body.
5. Consider how you feel when breathing. Notice if any part of your body is affected by negative energies. Visualize the healing effects of the bath, clearing up these problematic areas. If it helps, meditate before you delve into visualization.
6. Soak as long as needed, dipping your head under the water several times during your bath. When ready, exit the bathtub and dry yourself. Use a moisturizing agent after your cleansing bath.
7. If you've used only natural ingredients in your bath, take some bath water and offer it back to nature. Thank it for its help in cleansing you of negative energies. You can pour it into your garden or pots for your houseplants.

Salt Water Bath to Ward Off the Evil Eye

Saltwater baths have plenty of benefits. They can relieve stress, pain, and fatigue, improve circulation, and cleanse the chakra system. They're known to draw out toxins from the body, exfoliate the body, reduce skin irritation, and heal minor injuries. A lesser-known effect of salt bath waters is their ability to ward off the evil eye. While sea salt is the most effective for this purpose, you can use coarse sea salt if you don't have it available. It's an incredibly simple and ineffective method to ensure you'll never be affected by this curse and mal-intent.

Ingredients:
- Rock or coarse sea salt
- Lavender or tea tree essential oil
- A bucket
- Lukewarm water

Instructions:
1. Pour water into a bucket until half full. Add the salt and a few drops of essential oils to the water. Stir until the salt has completely dissolved.

2. Stand in your bathtub and slowly pour the salt water over your body, from head to toe. Avoid getting water in your eyes. Feel how it's cleansing you of negative energies.
3. Once you've finished with the salt bath, wash your hair and body with natural soap and shampoo. The salt can dry out your skin and hair, so you must replenish the nutrients-moisture immediately after the bath.
4. You can repeat the bath 2-3 times a week, depending on how strong your defense needs to ward off the evil eye.

Chakra-Balancing Ritual Bath

Balancing the energies in your chakras is crucial for attaining optimal spiritual health. You can balance your chakra bath and improve its energy-flowing capacities with a customized chakra bath. Use crystals, oils, and herbs associated with the chakra you want to balance. It's recommended to focus on balancing one chakra at a time.

Ingredients:

- Stones associated with a specific chakra
- Herbs linked to different chakras
- 8-10 drops of essential oils associated with a specific chakra
- 1 cup of Epsom or Himalayan salt
- Candles
- Colored light bulbs (optional)
- Music to relax (optional)

Instructions:

1. Cleanse your crystals before placing them on the edge of the tub. Clean them by smudging, putting them into a bowl of salt, or leaving them outside your window at full moon.
2. If you're using dried herbs, brew a strong tea with them first.
3. When ready, run the bath. If the stones are small, put them in a small pouch when placing them on the tub's edge so you don't lose them.
4. Place candles around the tub and light them. Put on relaxing music if it helps you calm down so you can focus on your cleansing intent.

5. Add the oils, salt, and herbal teas to the water and stir to combine. When everything is combined, get in, and enjoy your bath.

Pain-Pain-Go-Away Bath

Dealing with constant pain and fatigue negatively affects your chakras and your spiritual balance. You can restore your energetic balance and improve your overall health with a bath designed to make your aches go away.

Ingredients:
- Essential oils - chamomile, lavender, and rosemary work best or
- Dried herbs in infusion bags or fresh herbs
- Honey
- Oat milk
- Rice
- Dead sea salt
- Exfoliant for body and face

Instructions:
1. Fill your bathtub. Adjust the water temperature to your preference. While the tub is filling up, prepare the rest of the ingredients.
2. Mix 10-20 drops of essential oil and the rest of the ingredients in a medium bowl. Scale the ingredients according to your preferences, but you should create a homogeneous mixture.
3. Add the mixture to your bath and stir the water for even distribution. Get in and enjoy soaking for at least 20 minutes.
4. Before getting out, use an exfoliant on your body and face to deep clean your skin and activate a healthy flow of positive energy in your body, mind, and soul.

Rejuvenating Bath

There is nothing better than feeling refreshed after a spiritual bath. This bath will make you feel spiritually cleansed, rejuvenated, and ready to take on any challenges. It uses a special ingredient - wine. This beverage is packed with polyphenols, which are potent antioxidants. To truly relax while taking this bath, you can sip a glass of wine while soaking.

Ingredients:
- Essential oils - orange, lemon, sandalwood, and myrrh are best
- 1 glass of wine - plus one more to drink
- Lemon and orange rind
- Cinnamon sticks
- Fresh rosemary
- Dried roses
- Grapefruit juice
- Oregano

Instructions:
1. Fill in your tub with water and adjust the temperature to your preference. Prepare the other ingredients while you wait for the tub to fill up.
2. Add everything to the water (except the wine you'll drink) and stir to combine. If you're using loose, dried herbs, put them in a reusable teabag or cheesecloth to avoid clogging your drain.
3. After soaking for 20-25 minutes, do a good exfoliation to further boost your cleansing from the inside out. The massage will enhance the purification properties of the flowers and the antioxidants.
4. Once you have finished, air dry or gently tap yourself dry with a towel. Don't forget to moisturize after your bath to nourish your skin and seal in all the positive energies you've soaked up from the water.

A Spiritual Bath for Improving Energy Flow

This spiritual bath is designed to boost the energy flow through the entire chakra system. You'll be cleansed of negative energies and restore your physical, mental, and spiritual health. It is a combined approach of relaxation and circulation-boosting, enabling better energy flow.

Ingredients:
- Essential oils - chamomile, juniper, cypress lavender, and lemon are best
- Dead sea salt

- A neutral gel
- Honey
- Exfoliant

Instructions:
1. Fill your bathtub, adjusting the water temperature to your preference. Ideally, the temperature should be around 84,2-100,4 degrees Fahrenheit.
2. Add the essential oils to the bath, followed by gel, honey, and sea salt. Adjust the quantities to your preference.
3. Spend at least 20 minutes soaking and relaxing. Before getting out, do a complete exfoliation, massaging your body. This is key for improving blood, lymphatic, and energy circulation.
4. After getting out of the bath, air dry your body. Once you're dry, apply a nourishing oil to seal in the herbs' cleansing effects.

Bath for Unblocking Your Chakras

A nice, calming bath can do wonders for clearing out obstructions from your chakras. It re-establishes a healthy energy flow and balance in your body, mind, and spirit. For the best effects, it's recommended to take this bath strictly for relaxation purposes. Take a quick shower beforehand if you need to clean yourself, so you can focus on your intent to clear out chakra blockages.

Ingredients:
- Himalayan sea salt
- Colorful flowers - you can use dried and fresh
- Candles
- Essential oils
- Incense (optional)
- Meditation material (sounds, music, guides, etc., optional)

Instructions:
1. Clear all clutter around the bathtub. You need a clean tub without distractions.
2. Fill your bathtub with water. Adjust the water temperature to your preference.

3. While the tub is filling, settle on an intent. For example, you can wish to cleanse all the chakras or one or two blocked chakras causing you problems.
4. Light the candles. If you prefer, you can also burn incense. Prepare the meditation material, if any.
5. Add the oils, salt, and flowers to the water, and stir. When choosing the flowers, use the color corresponding to the chakra(s).
6. Get into the bath and spend 20-30 minutes soaking. Spend this time in silence, listen to a guided meditation or music, or do whatever helps you relax in the bathtub.

Enjoy rejuvenating and stimulating your body, mind, and soul by removing negative energy from your chakras with these spiritual baths.

Chapter 9: Crystal Purification and Protection

Have you ever felt like negative energy is weighing you down, and you can't seem to shake it off? Or maybe you've been in situations leaving you feeling vulnerable and unprotected. There are various methods to consider for cleansing and protection, but have you ever considered the power

Crystals are powerful tools for cleansing your spirit.[85]

of crystals and stones? Have you ever held a crystal or stone and felt a sense of calm or energy wash over you? Perhaps you've seen them in a store or online and wondered about their purpose beyond being a beautiful accessory. Crystals and stones have been used for centuries for their spiritual and healing properties, and they can be a great additional tool to your cleansing and protection methods. Each crystal carries unique energy and can help ward off negative energy, absorb it, or transform it into something positive.

In recent years, crystals and stones have gained popularity for their ability to aid in cleansing and protection. As life becomes more fast-paced and the surroundings more chaotic, people look for ways to maintain balance and harmony. Crystals can help to achieve this balance. This chapter explores the world of crystals and stones for purification and protection, from amethyst to black tourmaline. Each crystal carries unique energy and can help you on your journey toward inner peace and protection from negative energy. So, delve into the spiritual meanings of each crystal and how they can benefit you in your daily life. With the right crystals, you can create a protective shield around yourself or purify your energy to attract positivity and abundance.

Crystals for Purification

Crystals can be incredibly useful for purification, which involves cleansing negative energy and restoring balance to your life. Here are some of the most popular crystals for purification and their spiritual meanings:

1. Amethyst

Amethyst is a beautiful crystal with a vibrant purple color, known for its powerful energy and ability to promote peace and calm. It has been used for centuries as a tool for spiritual growth, healing, and purification. It's often used to transform negative energy into positive energy, making it a powerful tool for purification. Amethyst is often used to calm the mind, promote clarity, and aid spiritual growth. This beautiful crystal is associated with the crown chakra, the energy center located at the top of the head. This chakra is associated with spiritual connection, enlightenment, and the integration of the mind and body. One of the most common ways to use amethyst is to carry it with you as a piece of jewelry or a small stone in your pocket. Carrying it with you allows you to benefit from the crystal's energy throughout the day. You can place amethyst in your home or workspace to promote peaceful and calming energy.

2. Clear Quartz

Clear quartz is one of the most versatile and popular crystals available. Its clear and transparent appearance makes it known for amplifying and magnifying energy, making it a powerful tool for spiritual growth and transformation. Clear quartz has long been used to purify and cleanse energy. It's often called the "*master healer*" due to its ability to amplify the energy of other crystals, remove negative energy, and promote positivity. Clear quartz is associated with the crown chakra, which enhances spiritual connection, enlightenment, and higher consciousness. It can help balance and harmonize the chakras, promoting overall balance and well-being. Clear quartz can be used in numerous ways to promote spiritual growth and purification. One common way is to place the quartz in a room to promote clarity and positivity. It can be used in meditation to enhance intuition and promote inner peace. Clear quartz is used in energy healing practices, like Reiki, to help balance and harmonize the chakras and promote overall well-being.

3. Rose Quartz

Rose quartz is a beautiful and gentle crystal known for its ability to promote love, compassion, and emotional healing. Its soft pink color is associated with the heart chakra, the energy center located in the chest. This chakra is associated with emotional balance, love, and connection. The rose quartz's purpose is to promote emotional healing and encourage self-love and compassion. It can help release negative emotions and replace them with love and positivity. Rose quartz is believed to have a calming effect on the mind and body, reducing stress and promoting inner peace. One of the most common ways to use rose quartz is by placing it near the bed or under the pillow to promote peaceful and restful sleep. It is often used in meditation to promote emotional healing and self-love. Holding a piece of rose quartz in your hand during meditation can help connect with its energy and promote love and compassion.

4. Selenite

Selenite is a truly unique crystal that stands out from other purifying crystals due to its distinctive properties. One of the most remarkable properties of selenite is its ability to cleanse and purify not only other crystals but also spaces and environments. Selenite is believed to have the power to remove negative energy, blockages, and stagnant energy from the aura and the environment, leaving lightness and clarity. Unlike other crystals, selenite does not need to be cleansed or charged. It's known for its self-cleansing properties and is believed to cleanse and recharge other crystals in its proximity. It can help clear mental fog and promote mental clarity, making it an excellent choice for those seeking greater focus and insight. Selenite is a high-vibration crystal that can help connect to higher realms of consciousness and spiritual growth. It's associated with the crown chakra and promotes spiritual awakening and deep meditation. Selenite helps enhance psychic abilities and intuition, making it a popular choice for those interested in spiritual development and divination.

5. Carnelian

Carnelian is a beautiful crystal prized for its unique properties for centuries. It's believed to have powerful cleansing properties, particularly with the sacral chakra. This energy center is located just below the navel and is associated with creativity, passion, and pleasure. In addition to its ability to purify and cleanse the sacral chakra, carnelian is associated with several other properties. It promotes vitality, courage, and motivation, making it an excellent choice for those seeking to take action and make positive life changes. One of the unique things about Carnelian is its ability to remove creative blockages and promote inspiration and passion. It helps open up the creative energy flow, allowing for greater expression and a deeper connection with the creative self. Carnelian can be used in many ways to promote purification and cleansing. Some people wear carnelian as jewelry, like a necklace or bracelet, to keep it close and promote its unique properties throughout the day. Others place carnelian in a bowl of water to create an elixir ingested for its unique properties.

6. Celestite

Celestite is a stunning crystal that has long been revered for its unique properties. It's believed to have powerful cleansing abilities, particularly for the throat chakra. This energy center is associated with communication and self-expression, and celestite can help remove obstructions and promote clear communication. In addition to its cleansing properties, celestite promotes calm and tranquility. It's associated with the higher chakras, particularly the third eye and crown chakras, associated with intuition and spiritual connection. Many people use celestite in meditation or spiritual practices to promote inner harmony and connection with the divine. It helps remove negative energy and promote well-being, making it an excellent choice for those seeking to promote overall purification and cleansing. You can use it in a crystal grid or place it on your chakra during meditation to promote its unique properties throughout the body.

Crystal Combinations

Several combinations work particularly well when using crystals for purification and cleansing purposes. These combinations are often chosen based on the crystal's specific properties and how they complement and enhance one another. Some examples include:

- **Amethyst and clear quartz:** Amethyst promotes spiritual growth and clears negative energy. Clear quartz amplifies the other crystals' energy and promotes clarity and focus. Together, these two crystals can help remove negative energy and promote inner peace and clarity.

- **Carnelian and citrine:** Carnelian is associated with creativity and vitality, while citrine transforms negative energy into positivity and abundance. Together, these two crystals can help remove negative energy and promote creative flow and abundance.
- **Selenite and rose quartz:** Selenite is associated with cleansing and clarity, while rose quartz promotes love and compassion. Together, these two crystals can help remove negative energy and promote emotional balance and well-being.
- **Citrine and pyrite:** Citrine is known to attract abundance and promote positivity, while pyrite enhances manifestation and promotes success. Together, these two crystals can help amplify your manifestation energy and bring your goals and desires to fruition.
- **Quartz and selenite:** Clear quartz amplifies energy and promotes clarity, whereas selenite cleanses and purifies energy. When combined, these crystals help clear and purify your energy field, leaving you feeling refreshed and revitalized.

Crystals for Protection

Using crystals for protection presents a wide range of options. Every crystal possesses a distinctive energy and unique properties, aiding in building a protective shield around the wearer. Certain crystals excel in safeguarding against negative energy, while others offer physical protection against harm.

1. Black Tourmaline

Black tourmaline is a powerful crystal with properties making it an excellent choice for protection. It repels negative energy and provides grounding and stability to the wearer. This crystal is known for its protection against psychic attacks, negative entities, and other harmful energies in the environment. Incorporating black tourmaline into your life for protection can be done in several ways. One way is to wear it as jewelry, like a pendant, bracelet, or earrings, allowing you to carry its protective properties wherever you go. You can place black tourmaline around your home or workplace to create a protective barrier against negative energy.

When using black tourmaline for protection, keeping it cleansed and charged is important. Placing it in sunlight or moonlight or smudging it with sage or other cleansing herbs helps clear the absorbed negative energy and restore its protective properties. Black tourmaline is particularly effective when used in combination with other protective crystals. For example, combining it with smoky quartz can create a powerful shield against negative energy. It can be used with clear quartz to amplify its protective properties and create an even stronger protective barrier.

2. Citrine

Citrine is a warm and vibrant crystal often associated with prosperity and abundance. However, it has potent protective properties, making it an excellent addition to your protection toolkit. This crystal is known for transmuting negative energy into positive energy, helping create a positivity shield around the wearer. One of the unique properties of citrine is promoting mental clarity and focus. It is particularly useful when dealing with stressful or challenging situations, as it calms the mind and reduces anxiety or overwhelms.

Incorporating citrine into your life for protection can be done in various ways. One of the most effective ways is to carry it with you as a talisman or amulet. It allows you to always access its protective energy, no matter where you are. Citrine can be placed around the home or workplace to create a protective barrier against negative energy. When using citrine for protection, keeping it cleansed and charged is essential. Place it in sunlight or moonlight, or smudge it with sage or other cleansing herbs. Citrine can be used with other protective crystals for even greater effectiveness.

3. Black Jade

Black jade is a powerful crystal known to protect you from negative people and the energies they manifest. This crystal allows you to access your intuition and protect yourself from negative energies and situations. People often find it challenging to pinpoint the source of negativity; black jade is efficient for this purpose. It can help you find the root cause of negativity and protect you and your loved ones. Black jade crystal strengthens the connection to your intuition and gives you heightened awareness. This crystal can help you make decisions for your highest good to navigate life with confidence and clarity. Carry it with you to make the most of black jade's energy and to protect your energy from negativity. It is especially helpful when traveling or embarking on new adventures since the various energies you encounter can be unfamiliar and potentially challenging. To use this crystal in a protective ritual, place the crystal in your hand and set your intention. Keep the crystal in your pocket or wear it as a necklace when you've set the intention. Whether worn as jewelry or kept in your pocket, black jade is a reminder of your inner strength and resilience, helping you face life's challenges with grace and courage.

4. Hematite

Hematite is a protective crystal with unique grounding energy to help shield its wearer from negative influences. This mineral is known for its metallic luster and deep black color, giving it a strong and powerful presence. The purpose of hematite as a protective crystal is to create a barrier between the wearer and negative external and internal energies. It helps keep you grounded and centered, essential for maintaining a strong and protective aura. Hematite has been used for centuries for its protective and grounding properties, making it a popular choice for spiritual and healing practices. Incorporating hematite into your daily life can be as simple as wearing it as jewelry or carrying it in your pocket. Meditating with hematite is a powerful way to connect with its energy and strengthen your aura.

5. Labradorite

Labradorite is a mystical and protective crystal with a mesmerizing play of iridescent colors that catch the light and shimmer like magic. Its unique energy is known to ward off negative energy and protect its wearer from harm. The purpose of labradorite as a protective crystal is to help shield its wearer from unwanted energies trying to penetrate its aura. Its captivating colors calm the mind, making maintaining a positive and protective mindset easier. Labradorite enhances intuition and psychic abilities, making it a popular choice for spiritual practices.

Incorporating labradorite into your daily life can be as simple as carrying it with you as a protective talisman or wearing it as jewelry. Its energy is enhanced by holding it during meditation or placing it on your third eye chakra during a healing session. One of the unique properties of labradorite is its ability to protect and balance the aura, which is especially beneficial for empaths or sensitive individuals easily influenced by the energies of others. It can be used with other protective crystals to create a powerful energy shield.

6. Cat's Eye

Cat's Eye is a fascinating, protective crystal highly regarded for its unique ability to ward off evil and unseen danger. Its name comes from the distinct band of light running through the center of the stone, resembling a cat's eye. The purpose of the cat's eye as a protective crystal is to provide safety and security to its wearer, especially during uncertainty or change. Its energy helps release fear and anxiety, allowing for greater courage and strength in challenging situations. It is a powerful tool for dispelling negative energy and protecting against psychic attacks.

Incorporating the cat's eye into your life for protection can be as simple as carrying it in your pocket or wearing it as jewelry. Like all crystals, it is important to regularly cleanse and charge the cat's eye to maintain its protective properties through smudging with sage, placing it in the full moon's light, or using other preferred cleansing methods.

7. Shungite

Shungite is a powerful and unique crystal believed to have exceptional protective properties. This dark, almost black stone is composed of carbon molecules called fullerenes, known for their ability to neutralize harmful substances and electromagnetic radiation. As a result, shungite creates a protective shield against the negative energy emitted by technology and modern devices. In addition to its protective qualities, shungite has a grounding and stabilizing effect on its wearer. It helps with emotional balance and promotes calm and relaxation, making it a popular choice for protection against stress and anxiety and spiritual practices requiring a clear and focused mind.

Shungite can be used in several ways for protection. It is often worn as jewelry, like pendants or bracelets, or placed in the environment as pyramids or spheres. It is used to create shungite water, which is believed to have powerful healing and protective properties.

Crystal Combinations

Choosing stones that complement each other's properties and energies is essential when combining crystals. Here are some crystal combinations that work well together for protection:

- **Black tourmaline and clear quartz**: Black tourmaline is an excellent stone for protection against negative energy, while clear quartz helps amplify its energy and enhances its protective qualities.

- **Hematite and red jasper:** Hematite provides grounding and protection, while red jasper enhances courage and strength, making it a powerful combination for protection against physical harm.
- **Shungite and pyrite:** Shungite is known for neutralizing negative energy, while pyrite is a protective stone warding off negativity and danger.
- **Citrine and tiger's eye:** Citrine absorbs negative energy and transforms it into positive, while tiger's eye promotes courage, strength, and protection.

As you explore the world of crystals for purification and protection, remember these are tools to support your intentions and inner work. Crystals can help create a harmonious environment and protect you from negative energies, but they are not a substitute for personal responsibility and self-awareness. Take the time to connect with each crystal, learn about its unique properties, and find the ones that resonate most with you. Experiment with different crystal combinations, meditate with and incorporate them into your daily routine. Remember, crystals are powerful allies, and with a little intention, they can help you create a more balanced, peaceful, and protected life.

Only a few crystals for purification and protection have been mentioned in this chapter. Research online or enquire at your local stores and discover the vast availability of crystals.

Chapter 10: Cleansing and Protecting Your Loved Ones

As you journey through life, you will encounter many obstacles and challenges, leaving you feeling spiritually drained and vulnerable. Fortunately, various tools and techniques are at your disposal to help you cleanse and protect yourself from negative energy. But what about the people you care about? Your loved ones are as susceptible to negative energy and spiritual attacks as you. In a world often chaotic and unpredictable, it's natural to want to shield your loved ones from harm and negative energy. This chapter explores ways to extend the protection you've learned to your family and friends so they can feel spiritually safe and secure.

You can apply the methods in earlier chapters to protect others from negative energies; you merely need to modify the techniques to suit, whether a bath for your pets or children or a meditation session to help them find peace and security. The techniques in this chapter are rooted in ancient wisdom and have been used by cultures around the world for centuries. Incorporating them into your daily life, you cultivate peace and security for yourself and your loved ones, no matter what challenges arise. These methods provide unique and powerful ways to keep your loved ones safe and spiritually sound, even when you're not physically with them.

Meditation

Meditation is a powerful way to connect with the divine and release negative energy. With a few modifications, you can use this technique to provide spiritual protection and cleansing for your loved ones. This meditation helps create a protective energy field around your loved ones and promotes peace and positivity.

- Find a quiet and comfortable space where you won't be disturbed. You can sit or lie down, whichever is more comfortable for you. Follow these steps:
- Close your eyes and take a few deep breaths to relax your mind and body. Visualize your loved one standing in front of you, surrounded by a beautiful white light. This light represents their spiritual purity and protection.
- As you visualize the light surrounding your loved one, imagine negative energy or emotions leaving their body and being absorbed by the light. See the light grow stronger and brighter with each breath, cleansing and protecting your loved one.
- Next, take a moment to focus on positive affirmations. Repeat the following phrases silently or aloud, whatever feels most comfortable to you:
    - *"My loved one is safe and protected at all times."*
    - *"Negative energy has no power over my loved one."*
    - *"My loved one is surrounded by love and positivity."*
    - *"My loved one is filled with light and positivity."*
    - *"I radiate positive energy and love to my loved one, strengthening their aura and protecting them from negativity."*
- Take a few deep breaths and continue to visualize the protective cocoon of light surrounding your loved one. Send positive energy and love to them, and know they are protected and safe.
- When ready to end the meditation, take a few deep breaths and slowly come back to the present moment. Take a moment to ground yourself and release the remaining negative energy.

- By using this meditation technique, you provide ongoing spiritual protection and cleansing for your loved ones. It's a simple yet powerful way to promote peace, positivity, and safety.

Candle Ritual

Candle rituals have been used for centuries to promote spiritual cleansing and protection. The best part is they can be performed in person or from a distance, making them versatile for promoting positive energy and warding off negativity for your loved ones. Choose a white or black candle for cleansing and protection. White represents purity and positive energy, while black represents grounding and protection. You can use different colored candles depending on the ritual's intention. Follow these steps:

- If you're performing the ritual in person, find a quiet and comfortable space where you won't be disturbed. Sit or stand in front of your loved one, holding the candle in your hand. Light the candle and visualize your loved one if you're performing the ritual from afar.
- Light the candle, and imagine the flame representing the power of spiritual cleansing and protection. Hold the candle up to your loved one, and imagine the light and energy of the flame flowing into their body and cleansing the negative energy.
- If you're performing the ritual from afar, imagine the candle's light and energy reaching your loved one and cleansing away negative energy.
- Next, you can incorporate positive affirmations to reinforce the ritual's protective energy. Repeat the following phrases silently or aloud:
    - *"I call upon the power of this candle to cleanse and protect my loved one's energy."*
    - *"My loved one is surrounded by a shield of positive energy, protecting them from negative influences."*
    - *"All negative energy is released from my loved one's body and mind and replaced by positive energy."*
    - *"I send love and positivity to my loved one, promoting a healthy and vibrant energy field."*

- Allow the candle to burn for as long as you feel comfortable, focusing on the positive energy exchange between you and your loved one. When ready to end the ritual, take a few deep breaths and slowly release the remaining negative energy.

By using candles for cleansing and protection, you promote spiritual well-being and provide ongoing protection for your loved ones.

Crystal Protection

Crystals can protect in many ways, including creating a protective barrier around your loved ones, enhancing their personal energy field, and promoting safety and security. As discussed previously, some of the best crystals for protection include black tourmaline, amethyst, and clear quartz. Follow these steps to use crystals to protect your loved ones:

- Choose a crystal that resonates with your loved one's energy and intention. Depending on what feels right for them, you can use one or several crystals.
- Hold the crystal in your hand and set your intention for protection. Visualize a protective shield around your loved one or their space.
- Place the crystal in a location where your loved one spends most of their time, such as their bedroom, living room, or office.
- Remind your loved one to connect with the crystal's energy and intention whenever they need protection.

In addition to protection and cleansing, crystals can support your loved ones in many other ways. Here are a few ideas:

- **Meditation:** Encourage your loved one to hold a crystal while meditating to enhance the connection with their inner self.
- **Jewelry:** Giving your loved one a crystal necklace, bracelet, or earrings can give them the crystal's energy throughout the day.
- **Grids:** You can create a crystal grid by placing several crystals in a specific pattern to manifest a particular intention, such as healing, abundance, or love.
- **Bathing:** Add crystals to your loved one's bath to promote relaxation and cleansing.

Smudging

Smudging is a powerful way to protect and cleanse the energy of your loved ones, but you can make it even more personalized by creating a special smudging bundle specifically for them. Follow these steps:

- Gather a variety of herbs and flowers that resonate with your loved one's energy and intentions. You can include sage, rosemary, lavender, rose petals, or other herbs or flowers that hold special meaning for them. You'll need natural string or twine to tie the bundle together.

- Next, take a moment to set your intention for the smudging bundle. Visualize your loved one and imagine them surrounded by a protective shield of positive energy. You can include positive affirmations, such as *"May this bundle protect and cleanse my loved one's energy."*

- Once you've set your intention, assemble the smudging bundle. Take each herb or flower and place it in a pile, holding the intention for your loved one in your mind. Once you have all the herbs and flowers together, wrap them in natural string or twine, tying them tightly to create a compact bundle.

- To use the smudging bundle, light one end and allow it to smolder. You can use a heatproof bowl or shell to catch the ashes. Move the smudging bundle around your loved one's body, fanning the smoke with your hand or a feather.

- When you have finished smudging, extinguish the smudging bundle by pressing it into the heatproof bowl or shell.

Spiritual Baths

Spiritual baths are a powerful way to protect and cleanse the energy of your loved ones, but choosing ingredients safe for sensitive skin is important. Before using new ingredients, it's always best to test a small skin area to ensure no adverse reactions.

- Fill a bathtub or large container with warm water, adding herbs like lavender, chamomile, or calendula for a calming and soothing bath or rosemary and peppermint for an energizing and uplifting bath. You can add Epsom salts or baking soda for an extra cleansing boost.

- For pets, choosing ingredients safe for their skin and fur is important. Avoid using essential oils or ingredients known to be toxic to pets, like tea tree oil. Stick to safe and gentle ingredients like oatmeal, aloe vera, or chamomile.
- For children, choosing ingredients safe for their delicate skin is essential. Avoid using ingredients like strong essential oils that could cause irritation or allergic reactions. Stick to gentle and nourishing ingredients like oatmeal, coconut oil, or lavender.
- Once you've added in your ingredients, invite your pet or child into the bath. As they soak in the water, offer positive affirmations to help them feel protected and cleansed. For example, you could say, *"May this bath protect and cleanse your energy, filling you with peace and love."*
- After the bath, gently pat your pet or child dry with a soft towel and offer them a comforting hug or snuggle. You can smudge the room with sage or palo santo to help clear lingering negative energy.

Protection Jar

Protection jars are simple and effective ways to offer your loved ones ongoing protection and positive energy. Here's how to make one:

Materials:
- Small glass jar with a lid
- Salt or sand
- Herbs and crystals for protection (suggestions: black tourmaline, rosemary, sage, bay leaves, cinnamon, cloves, or lavender)
- Paper and pen
- Optional: ribbon or twine for decorating

Instructions:
1. Set your intention for the protection jar. For example, *"May this protection jar offer ongoing protection and positive energy to my loved ones, shielding them from harm and negativity."*
2. Fill the bottom of the jar with a layer of salt or sand. This creates a base for your herbs and crystals to sit on.

3. Next, add your herbs and crystals. Choose items that resonate with the intention of protection, like black tourmaline for grounding and protection or rosemary for clarity and protection.
4. Write your intention on a small piece of paper and fold it up, placing it inside the jar on top of the herbs and crystals.
5. Close the jar tightly and decorate it with ribbon or twine, if desired.
6. Place the jar in a safe and visible location, like on a shelf or in the corner of your loved one's room. You can carry it with you for added protection.

Whenever your loved ones need extra protection or positive energy, you can hold the jar and visualize the protective energy surrounding them. You can add or remove herbs and crystals to adjust the jar's energy.

Salt Healing

Salt has long been used for spiritual protection, to create an energy shield to repel negative influences, and promote safety and well-being. You can use special sea salt in several ways or other salts for protecting your loved ones:

Materials:
- Sea salt or rock salt
- Small cloth or fabric bag
- String or ribbon

Instructions:
1. Set your intention for salt protection.
2. Place a small amount of sea salt or rock salt in a cloth or fabric bag.
3. Tie the bag closed with a piece of string or ribbon, creating a small pouch.
4. Hold the salt pouch in your hands, focusing on your intention for protection.
5. Visualize a shield of white light surrounding your loved ones, repelling negative energy or influences.

6. Place the salt pouch in a safe and secure location, like on a shelf or under a bed.
7. Hold the salt pouch in your hands whenever you need to renew the protection and repeat the visualization and intention-setting process.

Salt Protection

Salt protection can be a simple yet powerful way to create an energy shield around your loved ones, promoting safety and well-being. Regularly renewing the protection helps keep their energy clear and protected. Another way you can utilize salt protection can include:

Materials:
- Sea salt or rock salt
- Protective herbs of your choice (e.g., rosemary, sage, lavender)
- Small bowl or dish
- Your loved one's photo

Instructions:
1. Choose a space where you will create the salt protection circle. It could be your loved one's bedroom, living room, or another place where they spend a lot of time.
2. Sprinkle a thin layer of salt around the room's perimeter to create a circle. As you do, visualize a bright, protective light surrounding the room and your loved one.
3. Sprinkle the protective herbs into the bowl or dish, and place your loved one's photo in the center.
4. Place the bowl or dish in the center of the salt circle.
5. Close your eyes and visualize a strong, protective energy emanating from the bowl or dish, enveloping your loved one in a protective bubble.
6. When ready, open your eyes and say a positive affirmation.
7. Leave the salt protection circle in place for as long as necessary. You can refresh the salt and herbs as needed.

Protection Talisman

A protection talisman is a great gift for someone who needs to feel safe and secure. You can create a talisman using crystals or other objects associated with protection, like black tourmaline, onyx, or hematite.

Materials:
- A crystal or stone associated with protection
- String or wire
- Small cloth bag or pouch
- Optional: additional protective herbs or symbols

Instructions:
1. Choose a crystal or stone that resonates with protection, like black tourmaline, onyx, or hematite.
2. String the crystal onto a length of string or wire, leaving enough space at the ends to tie the talisman into a loop.
3. You can add other protective herbs or symbols to the talisman if desired. For example, you might include dried sage, rosemary, or a protective symbol like a pentagram.
4. Tie the ends of the string or wire together to create a loop.
5. Place the talisman in a small cloth bag or pouch and give it to your loved one.

Whether you're performing a spiritual bath or creating a protection jar, the intention behind your actions makes them truly powerful. Setting your intentions and working with the right tools creates safety and well-being for those who matter most. Of course, exercising caution and taking safety measures is essential when working with potentially dangerous ingredients like fire and herbs. But with careful research and mindfulness, you can create a beautiful and effective way to protect and cleanse your loved ones.

Glossary of Useful Herbs

Basil

Basil is one of the most versatile herbs for cleansing and protection. It has long been used for its spiritual connections, as many cultures, like the Hindus, believe it wards off bad energy and attracts good fortune. Beyond these beliefs, basil has been prized for its medicinal properties. It helps soothe inflammation, boosts the immune system, and improves digestion. In addition to its physical healing powers, many people use basil in rituals before bed or during gatherings to evoke peace, love, and joy among those present. The possibilities of using basil to boost your physical and mental health are endless. Adding basil essential oils to a warm bath or creating a powerful cleansing spray to spritz around your sacred space. Additionally, basil is safe for children and pets, meaning it's a great addition to many households. Flavor-wise, basil is one of the most popular herbs, adding a delicious kick of flavor to any dish.

Aloe Vera

Aloe vera is an incredibly versatile healing herb and plant with applications ranging from skincare and cosmetics to spiritual practices. It can be used externally to soothe sunburn and keep the skin hydrated, added to bathwater, or boiled as tea. It is even safe enough for children and pets, making it a great natural protective shield against environmental factors and toxins. Aloe vera brings an extra layer of energy cleansing throughout your home when burned in situ like a smudging ritual. Alternatively, you can simply place a pot of aloe vera on one or both sides of your front door to guard your abode. Its flavor also adds something unique to food seasoning - incorporate aloe into your meals for a taste sensation.

Sage

Sage has long been considered a holy, healing herb invested with protective and cleansing properties. Practically, sage is a tactile plant. It can be burned or used as herbal tea and infusions, added to baths for additional cleansing, or used as a seasoning. It's popularly used in households. Small bushels of sage can be kept around the house to promote happiness, keep evil energetics away, and clear negative vibrations. Further, to protect your children and pets from negative influences in the household (as some believe), place a few potted sages around the house. These plants are non-toxic, making them an ideal choice for home protection. Last but not least, sage remains one of the top choices for spiritual practices like smudging rituals due to its purported powers of "positive energy" clearance.

Mint

Mint is one of the most versatile healing herbs and plants. It can be burned, steeped in tea, or as seasoning for food and drinks, but more importantly, it has spiritual meanings, making it a great addition to cleansing and protection rituals. Many believe that keeping mint in your home will bring good luck. Adding a few mint leaves to a pot of water and allowing the aroma to permeate your space is said to ward off bad vibes. Including crushed mint leaves in your bath helps relieve relaxation and muscle pain. Mint essential oil can be applied topically or aromatically. If making tea with fresh mint is your cup of tea (pun intended), it provides important nutrients and spiritual meaning. Finally, if you have pets or small children, keep an eye on interactions with fresh mint plants, as they are more likely to cause reactions than the dried varieties. No matter how you incorporate mint into life for its energetic or physical benefits, you can enjoy its energizing effects any time of the year.

Vetiver

Vetiver, or *Chrysopogon zizanioides*, is an incredible healing herb with numerous benefits if used correctly. This aromatic grass is native to India and South East Asia and has long been valued for its many spiritual, physical, and mental benefits. As a cleansing tool, it can be burned to bring forth positive energy and clarity. It can be brewed in teas to aid relaxation and is an excellent choice for spell work and ritual baths. Suppose you want to keep your home safe from energetic disturbances. In that case, adding vetiver into a potted plant or directly into the earth of each corner of your home can create deep protection. Using vetiver with children or pets, taking extra caution, and diluting the product is important since it is strong in scent but otherwise perfectly safe for all ages. Additionally, many chefs like adding ground vetiver root as a seasoning for its unique herbal flavor.

Lavender

Since ancient times the herb lavender has been prized as a magical plant to enrich life in many ways. It is known for its wonderful scent and healing properties, making it impossible to ignore lavender's strengths. Practically, it can be used for everything from creating soothing oils and cleansers for mental clarity to the trendy popular use of dried lavender blossoms in sachets. It is believed to help with protection and purification spells and can bring good luck when added to charms or carried as crystals. As an added bonus, in small doses or concentrations, lavender is considered safe for children and pets. Whether you add fresh air to your home with lavender essential oils or gently place sachets around your office or home, embrace the cleansing power of this uniquely gifted plant's medicinal and spiritual properties.

Jasmine

Jasmine is a magical and healing herb with origins in ancient history. From the moment you catch its distinct fragrance, you can unlock a range of positive vibes. Several spiritual meanings are attributed to jasmine. These include protection against negative energy, enhanced mental clarity, and amplified love and devotion. Jasmine has numerous practical uses in cleansing and protection:

- You can burn dried jasmine essence in your home to clear the air while bringing in positive energy
- Mix it with lavender for ultimate serenity
- Apply a few drops on your pillow or blankets for restful sleep
- Make an infusion of leaves and drink it to purify your body

- Wear the flower around your neck to benefit from its medicinal properties.

Additionally, jasmine is generally safe for children and pets when used properly.

Thyme

Thyme is a healing and protective herb that has been around for ages. The Greeks of ancient times used it for medicinal purposes. It has a long history in spiritual practices associated with cleansing rituals, luck, and safety. Despite its traditional uses, thyme is still popular in modern life; you can burn it to cleanse a space or make tea. Thyme has numerous practical applications - add it as seasoning to your dishes or put some in a pot as a protective charm. Although thyme is always safe for adults, it should not be used as food seasoning for young children, and pets should be kept away from burning thyme as smoke could irritate their lungs. Thyme offers many wonderful benefits when used correctly.

Rosemary

Rosemary is an incredibly versatile healing herb and plant, used for many cleansing and protecting purposes. It is believed to bring good luck and protection into the home, protect from negative energies, and encourage purification. Besides its practical uses like warding off insects, transforming bathwater into a magnesium-rich soak, tea for headaches, improving breathing, and aiding digestion, it is often burnt as incense or used in charms to concentrate on life's tougher problems. Rosemary oil can be soaked into a cotton ball and diffused around the room. It is safe for children and pets. Other ways include carrying it on you for good luck or wearing it as a crown. Incorporating this ancient herb into your life could bring welcome peace during a time filled with technology overload.

Bamboo

Bamboo is much more than a plant - it's a multi-purpose healer. Carefully harvested and handled, bamboo can be an integral part of your spiritual cleansing routine. Bamboo is thought to absorb negative energy, leaving the space free of unwelcome vibes and protecting the aura from external negative sources. Keep a few stems around your home or office for wealth, good luck, and protection to incorporate bamboo into your practice. Place them in areas of heavy traffic like doorways to ensure everyone entering the home or workspace benefits from its calming energies, or tie seven fresh jade green stalks with a red ribbon and hide it in an out-of-sight corner for powerful protection from the outside world. Additionally, the scent of burning dried bamboo helps create a tranquil atmosphere indoors. Whether you opt for smudging or a loving display, using this mysterious healing plant definitely won't harm children or pets as long as you exercise caution when handling burning materials.

Peace Lily

Peace lilies (Spathiphyllum) are a beautiful addition to many homes and gardens. Many people do not realize that peace lilies are herbs and plants with healing qualities, perfect for cleansing and protection. Spiritually, peace lilies can help bring security, inner stillness, and harmony. Practically, these herbs and plants have a unique ability to rid an area of negative energies or generate positive vibes when used in ritual spells.

Usage tips include:

- Infusions made from the flowers or leaves for drinking.
- Use fresh sprigs over yourself or others for spiritual cleansing.
- Carrying the dried petals in a pouch to ward off bad luck.
- Peace lilies are safe for children and pets, but purchase them from reputable stores or nurseries to ensure they're organic, unprocessed, and grown without synthetic fertilizers or pesticides.

Eucalyptus

Eucalyptus is a healing plant with supernatural properties. Its spiritual meanings rest in its purifying, protective, and cleaning abilities, making it a must-have for your ritual practice. Burning it creates a fuller, stronger connection with the spirit realm. Practically, it's beneficial for potent aromatherapy and reducing anxiety or stress. Eucalyptus is generally safe for children and pets, but parental supervision is recommended due to the heat and vapors. If its consumption is desired, please consult an herbalist before seeking alternate ways of ingesting this powerful plant.

Conclusion

Spiritual cleansing is a journey toward inner peace and purity. It is a process of letting go of the negative energies holding you back and opening yourself up to the positive and healing energies existing within and around you. The path to spiritual cleansing is neither a one-time event nor easy. It is a continuous journey requiring patience, dedication, and a willingness to let go of the past to make room for the future.

The core of spiritual cleansing is that people are made up of energy, which can become blocked or stagnant over time. Negative experiences, emotions, and thought patterns can cause these blocks, manifesting in physical, emotional, and spiritual dis-ease. Engaging in practices and rituals to help release the negativity and reconnect with your true self is essential for clearing these blocks and restoring balance.

The journey toward spiritual cleansing begins with a willingness to examine your beliefs and behaviors. It requires an honest assessment of what is holding you back and a commitment to making positive changes. This process can be challenging, as it often involves facing difficult truths about yourself and your life. However, only by acknowledging and addressing these issues can you begin to move toward a place of healing.

You will encounter obstacles and challenges as you navigate the path toward spiritual cleansing. You may find old thought patterns and behaviors difficult to break, or that negative emotions crop up at the most unexpected times. However, perseverance and a commitment to your spiritual growth will make you stronger and more connected to your true self.

Remember, the process of spiritual cleansing is unique to each individual. There is no one-size-fits-all approach, and what works for one person may not work for another. You must find the practices and rituals that resonate with your soul and make them a regular part of your routine. With each step forward, you will shed layers of negativity and embrace the light within.

The journey toward spiritual cleansing is not easy, but it is a journey well worth taking. You restore balance and harmony to your energy by engaging in practices and rituals to help you release negativity and connect with your true self. This process will not happen overnight, but with dedication and patience, you can transform your life from the inside out. So, let this book serve as a guide and a source of inspiration as you continue your journey toward spiritual purity and enlightenment.

Here's another book by Mari Silva that you might like

Your Free Gift
(only available for a limited time)

Thanks for getting this book! If you want to learn more about various spirituality topics, then join Mari Silva's community and get a free guided meditation MP3 for awakening your third eye. This guided meditation mp3 is designed to open and strengthen ones third eye so you can experience a higher state of consciousness. Simply visit the link below the image to get started.

https://spiritualityspot.com/meditation

Or, Scan the QR code!

Bibliography

AloDreams. "11 Dreams About Childhood Home - Meaning & Interpretation." Accessed April 1, 2023. https://alodreams.com/dreams-about-childhood-home.html

Alodreams.com. "#19 laughing - Dream Meaning & Interpretation." Accessed April 1, 2023. https://alodreams.com/laughing-dream-meaning.html

Alodreams.com. "#98 Dreams about Detached body parts - Meaning & Interpretation." Accessed April 1, 2023. https://alodreams.com/dreams-about-detached-body-parts.html

Angel Number. "Tunnel - Dream Meaning and Symbolism." Last modified March 17, 2021. https://angelnumber.org/tunnel-dream-meaning/

Apsara. "Falling in Your Dreams - Interpretation and Symbolism." Symbol Sage. Last modified September 28, 2022. https://symbolsage.com/falling-in-dreams-meaning/

Apsara. "What Does It Mean to Dream of Drowning?" Symbol Sage. Last modified September 26, 2022. https://symbolsage.com/dream-about-drowning/

Barber, N. "What Do Dreams of Numbers mean?" Dreams Limited. Last modified October 17, 2022. https://www.dreams.co.uk/sleep-matters-club/what-do-dreams-about-numbers-mean

Barber, N. "What Do Dreams of Water Mean?" Dreams Limited. Last modified June 17, 2022. https://www.dreams.co.uk/sleep-matters-club/what-do-dreams-of-water-mean-2

Barber, N. "What Do Ghost Dreams Mean?" Dreams Limited. Last modified December 13, 2021. https://www.dreams.co.uk/sleep-matters-club/what-do-ghost-dreams-mean

Basalt Spiritual. "12 Spiritual Meanings When You Dream About Drowning." Last modified December 8, 2022. https://www.basaltnapa.com/dream-about-drowning/

BetterSleep. "Dream Journals Explained." Last modified September 13, 2022. https://www.bettersleep.com/blog/dream-journal/

Björklund, Anna-Karin. "Do You Remember Numbers In Your Dreams? Here's What They Mean." Mindbodygreen. Last modified March 7, 2020. https://www.mindbodygreen.com/articles/what-does-dreaming-of-numbers-really-mean-heres-what-to-know

Brown, J. "What Does It Mean if You Dream About Flying?" ShutEye. Last modified July 16, 2021. https://www.shuteye.ai/dream-about-flying/

Bulkeley, Kelly. "Jung's Theory of Dreams: A Reappraisal." Psychology Today. Last modified March 23, 2020. https://www.psychologytoday.com/us/blog/dreaming-in-the-digital-age/202003/jung-s-theory-dreams-reappraisal-0

Casale, Rebecca. "How To Remember Your Dreams." World of Lucid Dreaming. Accessed April 1, 2023. https://www.world-of-lucid-dreaming.com/how-to-remember-your-dreams.html

Chakraborty, S. "Dreaming of Laughing – Enjoy the Good Times of Your Life." ThePleasantDream. Last modified May 25, 2023. https://thepleasantdream.com/dreaming-of-laughing/

Cherry, Kendra. "How to Interpret Dreams." Verywell Mind. Last modified February 23, 2023. https://www.verywellmind.com/dream-interpretation-what-do-dreams-mean-2795930

Christian, A. "8 Stairs Dream Interpretation." DreamChrist. Last modified December 24, 2020. https://www.dreamchrist.com/stairs-dream-interpretation/

Christian, A. "9 Beach Dream Interpretation." DreamChrist. Last modified April 2, 2020.. https://www.dreamchrist.com/beach-dream-interpretation/

Christian, A. "10 Laughing Dream Interpretation." DreamChrist. Last modified September 19, 2020. https://www.dreamchrist.com/laughing-dream-interpretation/

Christian, A. "15 Church Dream Interpretation." DreamChrist. Last modified April 7, 2020.. https://www.dreamchrist.com/church-dream-interpretation/

Christian, A. "10 Amusement Park Dream Interpretation." DreamChrist. Last modified November 6, 2020. https://www.dreamchrist.com/amusement-park-dream-interpretation/

Christian, A. "Forest Dream Interpretation." DreamChrist. Last modified November 11, 2020.

https://www.dreamchrist.com/forest-dream-interpretation/

Cummins, Pamela. (2017, June 8). "12 Benefits of Dream Interpretation." Last modified June 8, 2017. https://pamelacummins.com/2017/06/08/12-benefits-of-dream-interpretation/

Daphne. "Dream Of The Amusement Park? 7 Fun Reasons." Daphne Den. Last modified October 19, 2021. https://daphneden.com/dream-amusement-park/

Derisz, Ricky. "How To Boost Your Dream Recall For Higher Creativity." Goalcast. Last modified June 4, 2022. https://www.goalcast.com/how-to-boost-your-dream-recall-for-higher-creativity/

Donovan, Melissa. "Journal Prompts for Dreamers." Writing Forward. Last modified June 16, 2020. https://www.writingforward.com/writing-prompts/journal-prompts/journal-prompts-for-dreamers

Dream Dictionary. "Church Dream Meaning." Last modified May 18, 2020. https://www.dreamdictionary.org/dream-dictionary/church-dream-meaning/

Dream Dictionary. "Dreaming Of Angels." Last modified November 4, 2021. https://www.dreamdictionary.org/dream-meaning/dreaming-of-angels/

Dream Dictionary. "Dreams About My Childhood Home." Last modified March 26, 2021. https://www.dreamdictionary.org/meaning/dreams-about-my-childhood-home/

Dreams, J. I. "12 Dream Interpretation Techniques to Understand Your Dreams." Journey Into Dreams. Last modified August 12, 2022. https://journeyintodreams.com/dream-interpretation-techniques/

Dreams, J. I. "City Dream Symbol Meaning." Journey Into Dreams. Last modified July 22, 2018. https://journeyintodreams.com/city-dream-symbol-meaning/

Dreams, J. I. "The Meaning of Colors: Color Symbolism in Our Dreams." Journey Into Dreams. Last modified July 16, 2020. https://journeyintodreams.com/colors/

Dream Meaning. "Fairy Dream Meaning Interpretation." Last modified July 13, 2019. https://www.dreammeaning.xyz/fairy-dream-meaning-interpretation/

Flo Saul. "Beach." Auntyflo. Last modified October 4, 2012. https://www.auntyflo.com/dream-dictionary/beach-0

Flo Saul. "Dream of Amusement Park." Auntyflo. Accessed April, 2023. https://www.auntyflo.com/dream-dictionary/amusement-park

Flo Saul. "Dream Of Childhood Home." Auntyflo. Accessed April 1, 2023. https://www.auntyflo.com/dream-dictionary/dream-of-childhood-home

Flo Saul. "Dreams About Animals." Auntyflo. Accessed April 1, 2023. https://www.auntyflo.com/dream-dictionary/dreams-about-animals

Flo Saul. "Dreams About Church." Auntyflo. Accessed April 1, 2023. https://www.auntyflo.com/dream-dictionary/dreams-about-church

Flo Saul. "Dreams About Drowning." Auntyflo. Accessed April 1, 2023. https://www.auntyflo.com/dream-dictionary/drowning

Flo Saul. "Dreams About Running." Auntyflo. Accessed April 1, 2023. https://www.auntyflo.com/dream-dictionary/dreams-about-running-meaning-interpretation

Flo Saul. "Dreams Of Earth." Auntyflo. Accessed April 1, 2023. https://www.auntyflo.com/dream-dictionary/earth-and-earthquake

Flo Saul. "Forest." Auntyflo. Accessed April 1, 2023. https://www.auntyflo.com/dream-dictionary/forest

Flo Saul. "Laughing." Auntyflo. Accessed April 1, 2023. https://www.auntyflo.com/dream-dictionary/laughing

Flo Saul. "Library." Auntyflo. Accessed April 1, 2023. https://www.auntyflo.com/dream-dictionary/library

Flo Saul. "Passages or Halls." Auntyflo. Accessed April 1, 2023. https://www.auntyflo.com/dream-dictionary/passages-or-halls

Flo Saul. "Uncover Hidden Dream Meanings." Auntyflo. Accessed April 1, 2023. https://www.auntyflo.com/dream-dictionary/countryside

Floyd, L. "4 Things That Our Dreams Tell Us about Ourselves." Landofsleep. Accessed April 1, 2023. https://www.landofsleep.com/blog/4-things-that-our-dreams-tell-us-about-ourselves

Forneret, Alica. "Dream of Running Meaning: 18 Scenarios." Last modified April 2, 2023. https://alicaforneret.com/dream-of-running/

Forneret, Alica. "Dreams About Ghosts Meaning: 13 Scenarios." Last modified January 17, 2023. https://alicaforneret.com/dream-about-ghosts/

Forneret, Alica. "Flying Dream Meaning: Spiritually, Psychologically & More." Last modified April 17, 2023. https://alicaforneret.com/flying-dream-meaning/

GoodTherapy. "Dream Analysis." Last modified February 2, 2016. https://www.goodtherapy.org/learn-about-therapy/types/dream-analysis

Home Science Tools. "Elements: Earth, Water, Air, and Fire." Last modified October 6, 2017. https://learning-center.homesciencetools.com/article/four-elements-science/amp/

Jiang, Fercility. "The 20 Most Common Animals in Dreams & Meanings." China Highlights. Last modified August 23, 2021. https://www.chinahighlights.com/travelguide/culture/dreaming-about-animals.htm

Jones, Walter. "Dream About Dragon: Meaning & Spiritual Messages Explained." Psychic Blaze. Last modified February 6, 2023. https://psychicblaze.com/dream-about-dragon-meaning/

Kari Hohne. "Anatomy and Body Parts." Accessed April 1, 2023. https://www.cafeausoul.com/oracles/dream-dictionary/anatomy-and-body-parts

Kari Hohne. "Animals." Accessed April 1, 2023. https://www.cafeausoul.com/oracles/dream-dictionary/animals

Kedia, S. "Dreaming about a library - Are You Actively Seeking Knowledge?" Last modified May 31, 2023. https://thepleasantdream.com/dreaming-about-a-library/

Kerkar, Pramrod. "Dream Therapy: Dream Interpretation, Why Do We Dream." Pain Assist. Last modified January 30, 2019. https://www.epainassist.com/alternative-therapy/dream-therapy-dream-interpretation-meaning-of-dreams-its-benefits

Kiran. "What Does it Mean to Dream About Running?" Dreams & Myths. Last modified August 24, 2022. https://dreamsandmythology.com/dream-about-running/

Kotiya, Madhu. "Dreams in colour." Deccan Chronicle. Last modified June 10, 2018. https://www.deccanchronicle.com/amp/lifestyle/health-and-wellbeing/100618/dreams-in-colour.html

Ladyfirst. "What does it mean to dream of 4 elements?" Last modified June 30, 2023. https://www.lady-first.me/article/what-does-it-mean-to-dream-of-4-elements,6343.html

Liquids & Solids Spirit. "Dream About Sinking Ship? (7 Spiritual Meanings)." Last modified August 24, 2022. https://www.liquidsandsolids.com/dream-about-a-sinking-ship/

Lou. "What Does It Mean When You're Dreaming of Falling?" A Little Spark of Joy. Last modified February 21, 2022. https://www.alittlesparkofjoy.com/dreaming-of-falling/

Malory, J. "Earth, Air, Fire and Water in Dreams." Dreaming.Life. Accessed April 1, 2023. https://www.dreaming.life/dream-themes/earth-air-fire-and-water-in-dreams.htm

Master. "Basic Body Parts Dream Meaning - Common 64 Dreams About Body Parts." Dream Meaning Net. Last modified April 23, 2015. https://dream-meaning.net/life/basic-body-parts-dream-interpretation/

The Messenger. "Dream about Running Down A Hallway." DreamsDirectory. Last modified January 24, 2019. https://www.dreamsdirectory.com/dream-about-running-down-a-hallway-meaning.html

Miller's Guild. "12 Meanings When You Dream of Running." Last modified December 13, 2021. https://www.millersguild.com/dream-of-running/

Miller's Guild. "17 Meanings When You Dream About Eating." Last modified January 6, 2022. https://www.millersguild.com/eating-in-dream/

Mitrovic, M. "Dreaming of a Dwarf – Meaning and Explanation." Dream Glossary. Last modified September 25, 2020. https://www.dreamglossary.com/d/dwarfs/

More, R. "What Does the Number 9 Mean in a dream?" LoveToKnow Media. Last modified September 14, 2022. https://www.lovetoknowhealth.com/well-being/what-does-number-9-dream-symbolize

Nikita. "City Dream Meaning And Symbolism." Luciding. Last modified December 12, 2021. https://luciding.com/city-dream-symbol-meaning/

Numberogy.Com. "#14 Supernatural Dream Meaning & Spirituality." Accessed April 1, 2023. https://numberogy.com/supernatural-dream-meaning.html/

Nunez, K. "5 Lucid Dreaming Techniques to Try." Healthline. Last modified March 22, 2023. https://www.healthline.com/health/healthy-sleep/how-to-lucid-dream

O'Driscoll, Dana. "Dreaming Primer: Lucid Dreaming, Dream Recall, and Exploring Dreamscapes for Creativity." The Druids Garden. Last modified February 4, 2023. https://thedruidsgarden.com/2023/02/05/dreaming-primer-lucid-dreaming-dream-recall-and-exploring-dreamscapes-for-creativity/

Olesen, Jacob. "Color Meanings in Dreams: What Does Dreaming in Color Mean?" Color Meanings. Last modified December 11, 2014. https://www.color-meanings.com/color-meanings-in-dreams-what-does-dreaming-in-color-mean/

Parvez, Hanan. "Dreams about running and hiding from someone." PsychMechanics. Last modified April 25, 2022. https://www.psychmechanics.com/dreams-about-running-and-hiding-from-someone/

Pentelow, Orla. "The Meaning Behind Drowning In A Dream Is Just As Scary As The Dream Itself." Bustle. Last modified August 18, 2021. https://www.bustle.com/life/what-does-it-mean-when-i-drown-in-a-dream-while-its-likely-youre-stressed-there-is-upside-12708547

Porter, Liam. "Dreaming of Falling And What It Means." Dreams Limited. Last modified May 18, 2022. https://www.dreams.co.uk/sleep-matters-club/falling-in-your-dream

PsycholoGenie. "What Do Dreams About Stairs Mean and How to Interpret Them?" Accessed April 1, 2023. https://psychologenie.com/what-do-dreams-about-stairs-mean

Regan, Sarah. "A Beginner's Guide to Dream Interpretation & 8 Common Dreams." Mindbodygreen. Last modified April 29, 2023. https://www.mindbodygreen.com/articles/beginners-guide-to-dream-interpretation

Simwa, Adrianna. "Eating in the dream - what does it mean? Dream interpretation." Legit. Last modified September 19, 2018. https://www.legit.ng/1191964-eating-dream.html

The Sleep Diary. "10 Common Dreams About Stairs and Their Meanings." Last modified June 3, 2022. https://thesleepdiary.com/dreams-about-stairs/

Steber, Caroline. "7 Dreams About Falling, Decoded." Bustle. Last modified June 8, 2021. https://www.bustle.com/wellness/dreams-about-falling-meaning-experts

Surolia, K. "Dreaming of Plants – Does It Mean Growth Like Plants in Life?" ThePleasantDream. Last modified June 8, 2023. https://thepleasantdream.com/dreaming-of-plants/

Tamara. "Laughter in a Dream – Meaning and Symbolism." Dream Glossary. Last modified December 8, 2021. https://www.dreamglossary.com/l/laughter/

Tommy, M. "What Do Tunnels Mean In Dreams? – Beginning of A New Chapter in Your Life." ThePleasantDream. Last modified June 21, 2023. https://thepleasantdream.com/what-do-tunnels-mean-in-dreams/

What Dream Means. "What Does it Mean to Dream About Childhood Home?" Last modified March 5, 2021. https://whatdreammeans.com/what-does-it-mean-to-dream-about-childhood-home/

Wille. "The Ultimate Guide to Dream Interpretation." A Little Spark of Joy. Last modified May 9, 2023. https://www.alittlesparkofjoy.com/dream-interpretation

(N.d.). Beadage.net. https://beadage.net/gemstones/uses/purification/

(N.d.). Nataliemarquis.com. https://nataliemarquis.com/how-to-sense-energy-for-healing/

(N.d.). Yogainternational.com. https://yogainternational.com/article/view/what-are-the-7-chakras/

"11 Signs You Need A Spiritual Detox & How to Make It Happen." 2015. Mindbodygreen. July 6, 2015. https://www.mindbodygreen.com/articles/signs-you-need-a-spiritual-detox.

10 easy ways to cleanse your home of negative energy. (2012, April 3). Mindbodygreen. https://www.mindbodygreen.com/articles/how-to-cleanse-your-home-of-negative-energy

6 crystals to protect yourself from toxic people & negative energy. (2020, February 11). Mindbodygreen. https://www.mindbodygreen.com/articles/crystals-for-protection

Anahana. (2022, September 1). How to unblock chakras in A few easy steps. Anahana.com. https://www.anahana.com/en/wellbeing-blog/how-to-unblock-chakras?hs_amp=true

Beabout, L. (2022, May 26). Good vibrations: Your complete guide to chakra meditation. Greatist. https://greatist.com/health/chakra-meditation

Bryant, M. (2022, June 13). 25 crystals for charging and cleansing your energy. Sarah Scoop. https://sarahscoop.com/25-crystals-for-charging-and-cleansing-your-energy/

Chapter 4 - moving into higher vibrations. (n.d.). Meditation Guide - Happiness Meditation.

Chee, C. (2021, September 27). 6 of the best crystals for protection: Meaning & how to use. Truly Experiences Blog; Truly Experiences. https://trulyexperiences.com/blog/crystals-for-protection/

Cho, A. (2015, June 17). How to smudge your house to invite positive energy. The Spruce. https://www.thespruce.com/how-to-smudge-your-house-1274692

Choice, C. (2020, August 18). 10-minute practice to ground, breathe, soothe. Mindful; Mindful Communications & Such PBC. https://www.mindful.org/10-minute-meditation-to-ground-breathe-soothe/

Christopher. (2015, September 13). Reiki Level 1 Training: What to expect and how to prepare. Chakra Meditation Info. https://www.chakrameditationinfo.com/reiki/reiki-healing/reiki-level-1-guide-to-reiki-practice/

Clarke, Gemma. 2022. "What Is Spiritual Cleansing? + the Top Cleansing Rituals to Improve Your Energy Field." The Yoga Nomads (blog). Julien. September 24, 2022. https://www.theyoganomads.com/spiritual-cleansing/.

Curtis, L. (2021, September 29). 10 healing herbs with medicine benefits. Verywell Health. https://www.verywellhealth.com/healing-herbs-5180997

D'costa, M. (2012, November 21). Smudging and how it helps to cleanse your aura. Times Of India. https://timesofindia.indiatimes.com/life-style/home-garden/smudging-and-how-it-helps-to-cleanse-your-aura/articleshow/12866742.cms

Elkhorn, V. (2019, December 12). Smoke cleansing as an appropriate alternative to smudging. The Alchemist's Kitchen. https://wisdom.thealchemistskitchen.com/smoke-cleansing-as-an-appropriate-alternative-to-smudging/

English, M. (2018, April 24). Healing plants you should surround yourself with. Martha Stewart. https://www.marthastewart.com/1527900/healing-plants-for-your-home

Estrada, J. (2020, March 6). 5 reiki principles you can use to create more ease and flow in your life. Well+Good. https://www.wellandgood.com/reiki-principles/

Everything you've ever wanted to know about the 7 chakras in the body. (2009, October 28). Mindbodygreen. https://www.mindbodygreen.com/articles/7-chakras-for-beginners

Feldmann, E. (2019, February 7). How to use crystals for protection at home. Penguin.co.uk. https://www.penguin.co.uk/articles/2019/02/how-to-use-crystals-for-protection-at-home-hausmagick

Ford, Debbie. 2018. "Is It Time to Take a Spiritual Cleanse?" Oprah.com. June 8, 2018. https://www.oprah.com/inspiration/is-it-time-to-take-a-spiritual-cleanse.

Fosu, Kimberly. 2022. "3 Signs You Need a Spiritual Detox Plus Ways to Do It." ZORA. January 18, 2022. https://zora.medium.com/3-signs-you-need-a-spiritual-detox-immediately-plus-ways-to-do-it-f8ecc9bbbf98.

Girdwain, A. (2019, April 14). Summon your inner strength and confidence with these powerful crystals for protection. Well+Good. https://www.wellandgood.com/crystals-for-protection/

Gleisner, E. (2002). Reiki. In Principles and Practice of Manual Therapeutics (pp. 175-183). Elsevier.

Haria, D. (2021, August 26). Spiritual Bath: Meaning, Rituals, Techniques, Benefits and More. F and B Recipes. https://fandbrecipes.com/spiritual-bath/

Haugen, D. (2021, February 10). A Ritual Bath For Balancing The Chakras. Mindbodygreen. https://www.mindbodygreen.com/articles/balance-your-chakras-with-a-ritual-bath

Heidi. (n.d.). Smoke cleansing around the world. Mountainroseherbs.com. https://blog.mountainroseherbs.com/smoke-cleansing

How to Raise Your Vibration By Sabrina Reber. (n.d.). How to raise your vibration. Blogspot.com. http://howtoraiseyourvibration.blogspot.com/2011/03/actively-meditating.html?m=0

https://link.springer.com/article/10.1007/s10902-011-9286-2

Humphreys, K. (2019, August 14). Chakra Visualisation. Com.au; Head & Heart Mindfulness. https://www.headandheartmindfulness.com.au/blog-items/chakravisualisation?format=amp

IARP. (2014, April 20). History of Reiki: Read about the origin and traditions of Reiki. IARP. https://iarp.org/history-of-reiki/

Jain, R. (2019, June 13). Complete guide to the 7 chakras: Symbols, effects & how to balance. Arhanta Yoga Ashrams. https://www.arhantayoga.org/blog/7-chakras-introduction-energy-centers-effect/

Jain, R. (2022, December 22). How to unblock chakras with meditation and affirmations. Arhanta Yoga Ashrams. https://www.arhantayoga.org/blog/how-to-unblock-chakras-beginners-guide/?utm_source=google&utm_medium=cpc&utm_campaign=16771375909&utm_content=&utm_term=&gclid=Cj0KCQiArsefBhCbARIsAP98hXSkoM5bTDFkXuDwWKURDcvyTDJrs42d8nocO4aLCBSzZO_PVGkfDlcaAtiGEALw_wcB

Johnson, C. (2021, July 6). Chakra meditation: Unblock the 7 chakras with guided meditation. Anahana.com. https://www.anahana.com/en/meditation/chakra-meditation?hs_amp=true

Judith, A., & White, A. (2022, March 18). The complete guide to the 7 chakras for beginners.

Kalra, P. (2022, August 20). Repeat these 5 principles of Reiki daily for your mind, body and soul. Healthshots. https://www.healthshots.com/mind/happiness-hacks/reiki-for-mind-5-principles-you-must-affirm-everyday-for-mental-strength/

Kurt. (2017, July 4). Finding your centre: Grounding meditation techniques. Earthing Canada. https://earthingcanada.ca/blog/grounding-meditation-techniques/

Kyteler, E. (n.d.). How to make A protection jar (ingredients & spell). Eclecticwitchcraft.com. https://eclecticwitchcraft.com/how-to-make-a-protection-jar-ingredients-spell/

laura. (2020, April 3). 3 incredible spiritual baths rituals to do at home during the quarantine. Hotel CoolRooms Palacio Villapanés Sevilla. https://coolrooms.com/palaciovillapanes/en/3-incredible-spiritual-baths-rituals-to-do-at-home-during-the-quarantine/

Lawrenson, A. (2017, September 3). Chakra meditation: The secret to feeling more calm and grounded? Byrdie. https://www.byrdie.com/chakra-meditation

Lieber, A. (n.d.). How to tell if your chakras are blocked and how to unblock them. Dailyom.com. https://www.dailyom.com/journal/how-to-tell-if-your-chakras-are-blocked-and-how-to-unblock-them/?aff=91&ad=1&utm_source=google&utm_medium=cpc&utm_campaign=PerformanceMaxUK&acct=9358138875&cur=gbp&campaign_id=17483841340&gclid=Cj0KCQiArsefBhCbARIsAP98hXRWn-q_X091H7X4ZcIgx6gY-PFd_sQd0aVthUlimGZyUyUZ1dcDzTUaAq0lEALw_wcB

Lieber, A. (n.d.). The 7 major chakras: What you need to know and how to work with them. Dailyom.com. https://www.dailyom.com/journal/the-7-major-chakras-what-you-need-to-know-and-how-to-work-with-them/?aff=91&ad=1&utm_source=google&utm_medium=cpc&utm_campaign=PerformanceMaxUK&acct=9358138875&cur=gbp&campaign_id=17483841340&gclid=Cj0KCQiA6LyfBhC3ARIsAG4gkF-_3FfS2jnc4id0bCiuycfcP_FYwo2hOBaq5r1Powt2Q7LPTFnvQKEaApEIEALw_wcB

Lisa, P. (2020, February 3). Art of meditation. The Art of Living Retreat Center. https://artoflivingretreatcenter.org/blog/everything-you-need-to-know-about-meditation/

N.d. Yogabasics.com. https://www.yogabasics.com/connect/yoga-blog/spiritual-cleansing/.

Nine-herb home protection talisman. (2015, November 11). Wiccan Spells. https://wiccanspells.info/nine-herb-home-protection-talisman/

Nortje, A. (2020, July 1). 10+ mindful grounding techniques (incl. Group exercise). Positivepsychology.com. https://positivepsychology.com/grounding-techniques/

Paul, N. L. (2016, March 27). Reiki for dummies Cheat Sheet. Dummies. https://www.dummies.com/article/body-mind-spirit/emotional-health-psychology/emotional-health/reiki/reiki-for-dummies-cheat-sheet-209093/

Prasetyo, F. (2022, May 15). How to raise your vibration: The ultimate guide on raising your vibe -. Lifengoal. https://lifengoal.com/how-to-raise-your-vibration/

Raypole, C. (2021, May 5). Metta meditation for mother's day.

Regan, S. (2022, April 26). How To Make Your Bath A Spiritual Experience: 16 Tips & Techniques. Mindbodygreen. https://www.mindbodygreen.com/articles/spiritual-bath

Reiki self-treatment. (n.d.). Cleveland Clinic. https://my.clevelandclinic.org/health/treatments/21080-reiki-self-treatment

Safa Water. (n.d.). Salt Water Bath: A Cleansing, Healing, And Nourishing Ritual For Your Mind And Body. Linkedin.Com. https://www.linkedin.com/pulse/salt-water-bath-cleansing-healing-nourishing-ritual-your-mind-

Smudging 101: Burning sage to cleanse your space & self of negativity. (2015, March 13). Mindbodygreen. https://www.mindbodygreen.com/articles/smudging-101-burning-sage

Stelter, G. (2016, October 4). Chakras: A beginner's guide to the 7 chakras. Healthline. https://www.healthline.com/health/fitness-exercise/7-chakras

The 3 levels of reiki: What are they & what do they mean? (2014, December 1). Mindbodygreen. https://www.mindbodygreen.com/articles/the-3-levels-of-reiki

The three degrees of reiki. (n.d.). Reiki-light.uk. https://reiki-light.uk/the-three-degrees-of-reiki/

Top 15 spiritual plants. (2020, December 24). Floweraura Blog. https://www.floweraura.com/blog/plants-care-n-tips/top-10-spiritual-plants

What are chakras? (n.d.). WebMD. https://www.webmd.com/balance/what-are-chakras

What is a Spiritual Bath, and Do I Need One? - Black Female Therapists. (n.d.). Blackfemaletherapists.Com. https://www.blackfemaletherapists.com/what-is-a-spiritual-bath-and-do-i-need-one/

Your guide to candle magic. (n.d.). Rylandpeters. https://rylandpeters.com/blogs/health-mind-body-and-spirit/your-guide-to-candle-magic

Yugay, Irina. 2022. "Eliminate Problems from within Using Spiritual Cleansing." Mindvalley Blog. November 25, 2022. https://blog.mindvalley.com/spiritual-cleansing/.

Zoldan, R. J. (2020, June 22). Your 7 chakras explained – plus, how to tell if they're blocked. Well+Good. https://www.wellandgood.com/what-are-chakras/amp

Image Sources

[1] https://unsplash.com/photos/j8a-TEakg78?utm_source=unsplash&utm_medium=referral&utm_content=creditShareLink

[2] https://unsplash.com/photos/fVUl6kzIvLg?utm_source=unsplash&utm_medium=referral&utm_content=creditShareLink

[3] https://unsplash.com/photos/FwF_1Kj5tBo

[4] https://www.pexels.com/photo/hands-of-crop-faceless-man-under-water-7457629/

[5] https://unsplash.com/photos/Orz90t6o0e4?utm_source=unsplash&utm_medium=referral&utm_content=creditShareLink

[6] https://www.pexels.com/photo/a-falling-woman-wearing-a-sheer-dress-5655150/

[7] https://unsplash.com/photos/r6LQc9feEZQ

[8] https://pixabay.com/images/id-1072821/

[9] https://www.pexels.com/photo/ocean-waves-1646311/

[10] https://www.pexels.com/photo/purple-wall-color-1293006/

[11] https://www.pexels.com/photo/lots-of-numbers-1314543/

[12] https://unsplash.com/photos/P7L5011nD5s?utm_source=unsplash&utm_medium=referral&utm_content=creditShareLink

[13] https://unsplash.com/photos/Z-6bfsa6rD8?utm_source=unsplash&utm_medium=referral&utm_content=creditShareLink

[14] https://unsplash.com/photos/AVJ321HJFl4?utm_source=unsplash&utm_medium=referral&utm_content=creditShareLink

[15] https://www.pexels.com/photo/a-woman-dressed-as-a-vampire-14395497/

[16] https://unsplash.com/photos/_VkwiVNCNfo?utm_source=unsplash&utm_medium=referral&utm_content=creditShareLink

[17] https://pxhere.com/en/photo/1394621

[18] https://pixabay.com/es/illustrations/meditaci%c3%b3n-espiritual-yoga-zen-6988318/

[19] Atarax42, CC0, via Wikimedia Commons https://commons.wikimedia.org/wiki/File:Chakra1.svg

[20] Atarax42, CC0, via Wikimedia Commons https://commons.wikimedia.org/wiki/File:Chakra2.svg

[21] Atarax42, CC0, via Wikimedia Commons https://commons.wikimedia.org/wiki/File:Chakra3.svg

[22] Atarax42, CC0, via Wikimedia Commons https://commons.wikimedia.org/wiki/File:Chakra4.svg

[23] Atarax42, CC0, via Wikimedia Commons https://commons.wikimedia.org/wiki/File:Chakra5.svg

[24] Atarax42, CC0, via Wikimedia Commons https://commons.wikimedia.org/wiki/File:Chakra6.svg

[25] https://pixabay.com/es/illustrations/corona-chakra-enrg%c3%ada-chi-2533113/

[26] https://unsplash.com/photos/V-TIPBoC_2M

[27] https://unsplash.com/photos/VsI_74zRzAo

[28] https://www.pexels.com/photo/close-up-shot-of-a-woman-having-a-massage-5573584/

[29] https://www.pexels.com/photo/crop-masseuse-with-hands-near-ears-of-woman-5240700/

[30] Chokurei.jpg: Stephen Buck The Reiki Sanghaderivative work: LeonardoelRojo, CC BY-SA 2.0 <https://creativecommons.org/licenses/by-sa/2.0>, via Wikimedia Commons https://commons.wikimedia.org/wiki/File:Chokurei.svg

[31] L orlando, CC BY-SA 4.0 <https://creativecommons.org/licenses/by-sa/4.0>, via Wikimedia Commons https://commons.wikimedia.org/wiki/File:Seiheki.jpg

[32] Juan Camilo Guerrero, CC BY-SA 4.0 <https://creativecommons.org/licenses/by-sa/4.0>, via Wikimedia Commons https://commons.wikimedia.org/wiki/File:Hon_Sha_Ze_Sho_Nen_Symbol.jpg

[33] Nathaniel_U's, CC BY 2.0 <https://creativecommons.org/licenses/by/2.0/>https://www.flickr.com/photos/nathan_u/13121698433

[34] https://unsplash.com/photos/x5hyhMBjR3M

[35] https://www.pexels.com/photo/close-up-of-crystals-6766451/

www.ingramcontent.com/pod-product-compliance
Lightning Source LLC
Chambersburg PA
CBHW051854160426
43209CB00006B/1301